Aguinaldos

Aguinaldos

Christmas Customs, Music, and Foods
of the Spanish-speaking Countries
of the Americas

Virginia Nylander Ebinger

SANTA FE

Sunstone books may be purchased for educational, business, or sales promotional use.
For information please write: Special Markets Department, Sunstone Press,
P.O. Box 2321, Santa Fe, New Mexico 87504-2321.

Book design ◆ Vicki Ahl
Body typeface ◆ Bernard Modern Std
Printed on acid free paper

Library of Congress Cataloging-in-Publication Data

Ebinger, Virginia Nylander, 1929-
    Aguinaldos : Christmas customs, music, and foods of the Spanish-speaking countries of the Americas
/ by Virginia Nylander Ebinger.
        p. cm.
    Includes bibliographical references and index.
    ISBN 978-0-86534-689-5 (softcover : alk. paper)
    1. Christmas--Latin America. 2. Spanish Americans (Latin America)--Social life and customs.
3. Christmas cookery--Latin America. 4. Christmas music--Latin America. 5. Spanish Americans
(Latin America)--Social life and customs. I. Title.
    GT4987.155E25 2008
    394.2663098--dc22
                            2008043286

WWW.SUNSTONEPRESS.COM
SUNSTONE PRESS / POST OFFICE BOX 2321 / SANTA FE, NM 87504-2321 /USA
(505) 988-4418 / ORDERS ONLY (800) 243-5644 / FAX (505) 988-1025

Dedicated to

Mary and Philip Apodaca
Carl and Timothy Ebinger
Justin Archuleta

And their parents and Uncle John

Contents

Preface

Nobody writes a book alone. I am indebted to many, from the first germ of the idea to the last stroke on the keyboard. Friends, colleagues, and family all encouraged the idea and often talked me through hard places.

Some helped try out recipes—Jane Sherwood, Abad Sandoval, Jennifer Yahn, Victor and Annie Apodaca, Mary Helen Fierro Klare. Mary Helen and Carol Meine served as first-readers and critics, giving valuable assistance and criticism. Jane shared her professional editorial skills as well as her culinary skills. Sofía Lopez-Ibor gave me the title for the book and always inspired me with her encouragement. Carolynn Lindeman provided valuable sources of information. Pilar Posada was always ready to answer the countless questions I had, as well as to share her own compositions and arrangements. Both Pilar and Mary Helen gave generously of their time in making suggestions for clarification and accuracy in my use of Spanish words and phrases. Without that help, this book would have been of much less value.

Others with direct knowledge of a specific country, especially its music, who shared with me included, besides Pilar (Colombia), Juan de Dios Gonzales (Bolivia), Digna Gutierrez (Nicaragua), Susan Park (Honduras and Peru), Carolina Humphrey (Dominican Republic), Patricia Arana (Uruguay), Dina Graetzer (Argentina), Carlos Abril (Cuba), David Elduayen (Venezuela, Ecuador), Cecelia Martinez (Mexico).

The friendly, helpful staff at Mesa Public Library in Los Alamos, New Mexico, were always ready, with good humor and great competence, to suggest sources, to find information for me, and to facilitate my frequent interlibrary loans.

And the internet—both a blessing and a curse. A blessing because it has so much information; a curse for the same reason. Sometimes conflicting information creates a problem, but it can usually be resolved with enough digging. I was able to get valuable data especially on the history and geography of the various countries from internet sources.

Notes to the Reader

This book began as a collection of Spanish language Christmas carols. Very soon I knew it had to be limited in scope, so the Spanish-speaking countries of the western hemisphere seemed a logical, manageable area. As soon as that became clear, other questions arose: Are all the Christmas traditions alike? How do the songs and traditions fit together? Should something else be included?

And so it came to be that the book would include, in addition to the carols, each country's traditions and special foods of Christmas. Then all that was lacking was a context in which to fit these things together. What was each country like? How were the customs of one country different from those of the others?

The structure then emerged: Preceding the discussion of its traditions there would be a brief capsule of each country's geography and history, its climate and population density, the makeup of its people.

One notices immediately that not all the countries of South and Central America and the Caribbean Islands are included. That is for the very good reason that not all of them are Spanish speaking. In Brazil, for instance, the language is Portuguese; in Belize it is English. Official languages for Guyana, French Guiana, Suriname respectively are English, French, and Dutch. Some attention is given to the native languages within various countries, but Spanish as the official language is the great common denominator.

What are *aguinaldos*? The word is known throughout the Spanish-speaking world, but it is defined differently by different groups of people. To some it is a small gift, usually candy or fruit, given to children who go from house to house during the Christmas season "begging *aguinaldos*," or the verse by which they ask for these treats. An *aguinaldo* can also be a gift of money to business employees or servants or to those who have performed other services during the year.

To others, though, *aguinaldos* are Christmas carols, dating from medieval Spain where groups of merry-makers, *parrandas*, came together to sing in the streets and to visit their friends for refreshments. Simple melodies usually in triple meter, *aguinaldos* sing the joy of Christmas, most often in secular expression. They appear to have come from Europe first to Puerto Rico, spreading from there throughout the area. They usually are accompanied by folk instruments.

There is by necessity some amount of repetition in the book. Since they share the same language and predominantly the same religion, it follows that the countries would share much of the same culture and tradition. I have tried to include always the unique ways of celebrating the holiday, but many times the same custom is observed in more than one country, hence some repetition with only slight variation—for example, many countries observe the folk custom of eating twelve grapes on New Year's Eve; many believe the color yellow has special power to bring good luck in the new year; all pay reverence to the Holy Family.

Spanish geographical names and names of persons are not italicized. All other words in Spanish are so marked. Each Spanish word is immediately followed, the first time it appears, by its English equivalent in parentheses. The Glossary contains definitions of all the Spanish words. You will note some differences in capitalization of words. Spanish makes much less use of upper case than does English. For instance, we Americans are *americanos* and the book title *Traditional Argentinian Villancicos* is *Villancicos tradicionales argentinos* Inconsistency in following their own rules, however, makes it hard on the researcher. I have tried to solve the problem by following the lead of the sources cited: for instance, some book titles are capitalized according to Spanish rules of capitalization, some are not.

The physical and cultural features of the countries are not covered in depth. This is less true for the sections on Mexico and New Mexico simply because I am a native New Mexican, I have visited many times in Mexico, and I have Mexican friends. I hope the short overviews of all the countries will stimulate your interest and lead you to your own research.

The Caribbean Islands

On Tuesday, December 25, 1492, Christopher
Columbus wrote in his log:
I sailed in a slight wind yesterday . . . and at
the passing of the first watch, 11 o'clock at
night . . .I decided to lie down to sleep because
I had not slept for two days and one night.
Since it was calm, the sailor who was steering
the ship also decided to catch a few winks and
left the steering to a young ship's boy. . . .I felt
secure from shoals and rocks. . . .Our Lord
willed that at midnight, when the crew saw me
lie down to rest and also saw that there was a
dead calm and the sea was as in a bowl, they
all lay down to sleep and left the helm to that
boy. The currents carried the ship upon one of
these banks. . . . Although there was little or
no sea, I could not save her.

Columbus had arrived in what he thought were the Spice Islands,
the Moluccas in the China Sea, on October 12,1492. His
first landfall, thirty-three days after leaving the Canaries, was
probably the small island we know today as Watling in the Lesser Antilles
in the Caribbean Sea.

He was greeted by friendly natives and, assuming they were in the Moluccas, he called them Luccans. He named the island San Salvador; its people called it Guanahaní. After several days of exploring the island and surrounding waters and trading with the natives—glass beads, red caps, and hawks bells for parrots, cotton, and spears—and observing the gold ornaments they wore, the Spaniards moved on, sighting Cuba which he named Juana and described as "fertile, temperate, level, and beautiful." Cuba's native people were frightened of Columbus and his men and at first fled from them, but the admiral instructed them to treat the natives kindly and to let them know nothing would be taken from them—except perhaps a little gold!

After exploring the waters around Cuba for several weeks, they set out for Bohío, entering on December 5 a bay he named for San Nicolás. He called the island Hispaniola. There he saw what he believed to be nutmeg and other spice trees, reinforcing his belief that he had indeed reached the Orient. It was on this island of Hispaniola that the luckless *Santa María* met its Christmas Eve fate.

The tiny *Niña* was not big enough for the entire crew to return to Spain, and The *Pinta* had gone earlier on another mission, so Columbus had little choice but to leave some of his men on the island among the friendly natives whom we now know were Taino peoples of the Arawak strain. Leaving enough supplies and arms to last a year, he instructed thirty-nine of his crewmen to stay, to build a fort, and to establish a *villa* which he named, appropriately, La Navidad; he and the others returned home to Spain.

His second voyage to this New World began in early fall of 1493. After visiting briefly other small islands as well as Puerto Rico, he returned to Hispaniola hoping to be welcomed by those he had left in La Navidad nearly a year before. Instead, he found no trace of the village, the fort, or the men, and Chief Guacanagari who had treated him with such hospitality, told Columbus that the men had argued among themselves over gold and women and some had abandoned the village. Others had raided an inland village and stolen native women. Tribesmen then retaliated by destroying the fort and killing all the remaining Spaniards.

But Columbus's mission was clear, and he pressed on. Encouraged by tales of the rich lands he had found, the royals of Spain equipped Columbus with seventeen ships, livestock, and more than a thousand men to begin serious colonization. The establishment at La Navidad lost, they settled a new colony and called it La Isabela on the northeast coast of present-day Dominican Republic, the eastern part of Hispaniola. Columbus served as colonial governor for several years, but while he held this position he continued his explorations, never giving up the belief that he was very near the mainland of China.

Columbus returned to Spain to seek more help for his colonies, and in March 1498 he began his third voyage to the New World he had discovered, his third attempt to sail ever westward to find the mainland of China.

But that is the story for the next chapter. Here we will consider the land, its people, and the Christmas customs of the island peoples of the Caribbean, the Greater Antilles Spanish-speaking islands of Cuba, the Dominican Republic, and Puerto Rico.

Cuba

The Land and Its People

Cuba, the largest of the Greater Antilles, is about the size of Pennsylvania. Shaped rather like an alligator, it is approximately 750 miles long and varies between 60 and 125 miles wide. It is situated where the Atlantic Ocean, the Caribbean Sea, and the Gulf of Mexico flow together. Cuba is just 90 miles from the Keys of Florida. Its population is about eleven and a half million.

After Columbus made first landfall at a small island he called San Salvador, he sailed on, stopping briefly and laying claim to two other small islands, and on October 27, 1492, he landed on the shores of Cuba. "I have never seen anything so beautiful," he wrote. He named it Juana after Prince Juan, King Ferdinand and Queen Isabella's son. Its natives called it Cubanacán.

Columbus and his men were met by native Taino, a division of the Arawak who inhabited most of what is today Central America. The Taino were a shy, gentle people who were hospitable to the Spaniards and engaged in trading after some initial fearfulness. This first group of Spanish explorers treated the natives with respect and friendship. Unfortunately, those who came later would treat them differently, and within half a century only a few of the natives had survived the harsh treatment and disease that had been dealt to them.

Diego Velasquez began the colonization of Cuba in 1511 and by 1515 had established a number of settlements including Havana, though that city was not named the capital until 1607. Slave trading, to augment the dwindling labor force among the natives, began in 1513, and slavery continued in Cuba until 1886.

Cuba was the last major Spanish colony to gain independence.

Except for a year in the 1760s when England invaded and captured Havana, Cuba remained a colony of Spain until the great hero José Martí began a rebellion in 1895 that lasted until 1898 when outright war between Spain and Cuba began. When the battleship *USS Maine* exploded in the Havana harbor—from causes mysterious to this day—the United States entered the war. The war lasted only a few months, and Cuba was ceded to the United States in trust for its citizens by the Treaty of Paris at the end of 1898. United States military rule lasted until 1902, when Cuba became a republic.

For the first half of the twentieth century the land was ruled by military dictators. A revolution in the late 1950s resulted in Cuba being declared a socialist state.

✱ Christmas Traditions

In 1969 Christmas was removed by the government from the list of holidays in the Cuban calendar, but in honor of a visit by Pope John Paul II in 1998, dictator Fidel Castro reinstated the celebration of Christmas in Cuba. Although nearly three decades of absence may have dimmed memories, many of the old traditions have come back to life.

Now, with the possibility of once again celebrating Christmas, thousands line the streets of Havana and crowd into Revolution Square where they listen to the peal of the church bells and attend the large outdoor mass on Christmas Eve. And always in Cuba there is music and dancing, especially so in this season.

In some places *parranda*s (parties with great revelry) as well as processions and competitions are held in the days before Christmas. Churches erect nativity scenes within their vestibules.

In times past it was the custom in many parts of the country on December 23 to kill a pig, clean it and hang it for a few hours, then to wrap it in banana leaves and place it in a marinade of orange, garlic, oregano, and pepper, and leave it overnight, cooking it slowly through the next day so it would be ready for Christmas dinner. This tradition remains alive in the Cuban population of Florida where *el lechón* (the pig) is placed in a makeshift barbecue pit called *la caja china* (the Chinese box) and rotated through the day, carefully watched over by the men of the extended families who are supported by fortified *bebidas* of *cerveza* or *ron* (drinks of beer or rum). Women meanwhile are busy in the kitchen cooking *moros y cristianos* (black beans and rice), *tres leches, flan,* and other tasty desserts. A nearby Cuban bakery will provide bread, pastries, cheese, and other necessities of the Cuban *cena de Navidad* (Christmas meal).

Christmas Eve dinner is the highlight. Families gather around the table for the roast pork and all the results of the women's cooking. After dinner comes the time for singing when all generations of the family gather around the *abuela* (grandmother) or other elders to sing *villancicos* and *tonadas,* those both from times past and contemporary times. Christmas Day is saved as a quiet time of reflection and visiting with loved ones and feasting again on the leftovers, *la montería.*

New Year's Eve is the occasion for more partying, another big dinner, fireworks. Some observe the custom of throwing twelve pails of water from their homes, signifying the passing of the old year, and eating twelve grapes to bring good fortune to the new year. It is a time for *brindis* (toasts), *abrazos* (embraces), *felicidades,* (good wishes), and then more music and dancing.

On the night of January 5, the eve of *Los Reyes Magos,* children prepare boxes of straw and containers of water for the Kings' camels, placing them where the Kings will be sure to see them, and then go to bed to await the morning's excitement—gifts and treats left by the Kings in exchange for the food and drink for their camels.

Dominican Republic

The Land and Its People

The Dominican Republic and Haiti share the island of Hispaniola, second largest island of the Greater Antilles. The Dominican Republic's portion, about the size of Vermont and New Hampshire combined, occupies the eastern two-thirds of the island, with French-speaking Haiti in the western third.

Evidence suggests the island had been inhabited for five thousand years before its discovery by European explorers. The Dominican Republic is a mountainous land with three major mountain ranges. Its highest peak and the highest in the Antilles, Pico Duarte, rises to an altitude of about 10,000 feet. It is a tropical country with an average annual rainfall of more than fifty inches and in some high mountain areas nearly twice that. Its coastline is outlined by both the Atlantic Ocean and the Caribbean Sea, and it is subject to periodic hurricanes in the summer and fall months.

Columbus's probable first landfall, on October 12, 1492, was a small island in the Bahamas we know now as Watling; its natives called it Guanahaní; Columbus named it San Salvador. After three days he made brief stops at two other small islands, then landed on the island of Cuba which he named Juana on October 27. After several weeks of exploring the interior as well as the surrounding waters, Columbus sailed southeast on December 5 toward the large island of Bohío.

In his log he writes, "At the hour of vespers we entered a harbor that I named Puerto de San Nicolás, in honor of St, Nicholas because it was his feast day. As I approached the entrance of this harbor, I marveled at its beauty and excellence. . . ."

He named this island Isla Española.

Here on the island we now know as Hispaniola comprising Haiti and the Dominican Republic, Columbus found hospitable Tainos who shared their food and were eager to trade with the Spaniards. As they explored the northern coastline of the island, they continued to be met by friendly natives.

On the night of Christmas Eve the seas were calm, and Columbus and his men, in preparation for their return voyage to Spain, slept in their ships moored near Cape Haitien on northern Hispaniola. But during the night ocean currents pushed the *Santa María* onto a reef and the ship was wrecked. Natives rushed to help the visitors, unloading supplies from the ship and offering housing to the men. These acts of kindness so impressed Columbus that he decided to leave thirty-nine of his men on the island, with sufficient supplies to last until he returned the following year, to establish a small settlement. He instructed them to build a fort from the timbers of the dismantled *Santa María*, and before he left he named the place, in honor of the date, La Navidad. Unfortunately, on his second voyage in 1493 he revisited the island to discover that all traces of the settlement had disappeared.

Bartholomew Columbus, brother of the famed explorer, established the city of Santo Domingo in 1496, the oldest European city in the New World and present day capital of the Dominican Republic. Unlike Haiti on the other side of the island, the Dominican Republic produced few major goods for export and therefore imported few slaves. It continued under Spanish rule for nearly three centuries. At the end of the eighteenth century it entered a difficult period of swinging back and forth between French, Spanish, and independent Haitian control until finally on February 27, 1844, under the leadership of its great hero Juan Pablo Duarte, it declared its independence and became the Dominican Republic. Today's population is more than nine million.

✲ Christmas Traditions

Las Navidades, the entire Christmas season, begins early in December and continues through January 6 in the Dominican Republic. It is a time for the gathering of family and friends for visiting, sharing festive meals, exchanging gifts. Every public employee receives a *doble sueldo*, a Christmas bonus equal to one month's salary. Most businesses also follow this custom with their employees. Small presents exchanged between friends or fellow workers are called *angelitos*.

Small groups of people, three or four at a time, singing and playing the Dominican Republic's special *merengue* music, appear throughout the month. Other groups sing traditional *aguinaldos* outside homes until the hosts open their doors and invite them in for refreshments—rum, coffee, or the typical *gingebre* (ginger punch).

A *charamico* can be found in many homes. This is a dry branch painted white, decorated with lights and ornaments, substituting for a Christmas tree, under which the *nacimiento* is built. Also common is the *flor de pascua* or *estrella de Navidad* which we know as poinsettia.

The traditional *cena*, served late in the evening, includes such things as grilled pork or ham, or *sancocho* (a soup popular at Chrstmas), *habichuelas* (red beans), and fruits. *Pastelitos*, meat-filled turnovers, are also a popular holiday food. Most attend *la misa de gallo*, the mass of the rooster, so named because it begins at midnight on Christmas Eve and ends in the early morning hours of Christmas Day, not long before the cock crows, and also because legend says the rooster was the first creature to announce the birth of the Baby Jesus. Dominicans are among those who eat grapes while making a wish for good luck in the coming year.

Christmas Day is a quieter time. There are some gifts for the children, but most of the gift-giving occurs on *el día de Reyes*, January 6. On January 5 the Three Kings parade through the streets. Children scream with excitement, shouting to the Kings to include any gift they might have forgotten to ask for. The children then rush home to prepare containers of grass and water for the Kings' camels before they go to bed in expectation of the exciting morning to come, for after their camels have eaten the grass and drunk the water, the Kings always leave gifts for the children in the empty boxes. On January 21 *la vieja Belén*, the old lady of Bethlehem, visits poor children whose parents could not afford an earlier Christmas gift.

Puerto Rico

The Land and Its People

Smallest of the islands of the Greater Antilles, Puerto Rico is not an independent republic but rather a territory of the United States with commonwealth status. The mountains in this small tropical island give rise to more than fifty rivers. It is the home of more than two hundred plant species, sixteen birds, and thirteen reptiles/amphibians, including the *coqui,* a tiny tree frog that sings from dusk to dawn.

On Columbus's second voyage in 1493 he found Puerto Rico whose friendly Tainos, a group of Arawaks, met him. They called their island Boriquén, (land of the great lords); Columbus named it San Juan Bautista. After this first encounter with the Spanish it was fifteen years before settlement of the island began. In 1508 Juan Ponce de Leon, who had been with Columbus in 1493, invaded Boriquén and set up the first colony at Caparra on San Juan Bay.

The hospitality of the Tainos turned quickly to fear and resentment with the establishment of the *repartimiento* system whereby each colonist was assigned a number of natives whom he would care for and teach the Christian religion in exchange for what became forced, slave labor.

Disease and difficult working conditions brought about decimation of the Taino natives so that by 1514 there were fewer than four thousand of the estimated thirty thousand to forty thousand who had occupied the island when the Spaniards arrived. To add to the dwindling labor force, Africans were imported in the early years of the sixteenth century.

Puerto Rico soon became a place of great value to Spain, and to protect its rich resources construction of the great fortress-castle of El Morro de San Felipe began in 1539. El Morro stood firm in later years when Sir Francis Drake and his fleet attacked San Juan and were repelled and when the Dutch under General Boudewin Hendricksz attacked and burned much of San Juan but finally retreated when they were unable to take El Morro.

Puerto Rico remained a colony of Spain until the end of the nineteenth century. At the beginning of the Spanish American War in 1898 the United States invaded Puerto Rico, and at the war's end, under the Treaty of Paris, it, along with Cuba, was transferred to United States territorial ownership. Puerto Ricans were made United States citizens in 1917 and have been allowed to elect their own governor since 1948.

Its population of nearly four million comprises those of African or Spanish ancestry and the Taino/Spanish mestizos known as jíbaros, rural dwellers with strong Spanish roots, noted for their music.

⁑ Christmas Traditions

La Navidad is a long season in Puerto Rico, beginning in early December and continuing through the middle of January. A tradition of longstanding is the *parranda*, also known as *asalto* or *trulla*, which is Christmas caroling Puerto Rican style. Groups of singers and players gather in late evening in front of a chosen house, waking and surprising those inside with *aguinaldos*. The musicians are invited in for an impromptu party after which the hosts join the *parranderos* as they go to another house to repeat the process. This goes on from house to house, the group constantly growing, until the early morning hours.

Early morning *misas de aguinaldo* occur on the nine days preceding *Nochebuena* (Christmas Eve). *La misa de gallo* is held at midnight on Christmas Eve. The lavish Christmas dinner can come either before or after mass. Typically the meal features *pasteles* (pastries), *arroz con dulce* (sweetened rice), *tembleque* and *coquito* (puddings), and especially roast pork that has been ceremonially prepared in the *lechón asao*. This all-day party starts very early in the morning when a newly slaughtered pig is placed on a spit and cooked slowly over coals throughout the day. Of course the event is filled with lots of Christmas music and general jollity.

The next important day is December 28, *el día de los inocentes,* a time for friends and family to play tricks on one another. An old tradition from the Canary Islands, the ancestral homeland of many jíbaros, is a kind of carnival in which "Herod's soldiers" kidnap first-born sons who can be redeemed with gifts of candy and sweets.

Friends gather again on December 31 to observe *la despedida del año* (farewell to the old year). This is the occasion to hug and toast each other, to listen to the reading of a special poem written for the occasion, to say goodbye to the old year and wish for good luck in the coming year which is invited by eating twelve grapes as the clock bells toll midnight, and throwing out the window bad luck in a pail of water. It is important to have everything very clean—houses, cars, streets—because the way the new year finds them is the way they will remain all year.

At last, to the children's joy, comes *el día de Reyes,* the day the Kings have left their gifts in exchange for the grass and water the children have left for the Kings' camels.

But this is not the end. Still to come are *las octavitas* immediately following the feast days of the Kings, Gaspar on January 6, Melchor on January 7, and Baltasar on January 8. The next eight days are celebrated in a carnival atmosphere of continued *parrandas* that include lots of singing and dancing and feasting to celebrate the Kings' journey from far lands in the East to Bethlehem to worship the Baby Jesus.

South America

A vast and diverse landmass, South America is the fourth largest continent in area, fifth in population. It is a land of extremes—the world's highest waterfall: Angel Falls in Venezuela; the longest mountain range: the Andes in Argentina, Bolivia, Chile, Colombia, Ecuador, Perú, and Venezuela; the largest river and the largest rainforest: the Amazon; the driest desert: Atacama in Chile, Perú, and Bolivia; the highest capital city: La Paz, Bolivia; the most southern town: Puerto Toro, Chile.

The Spanish-speaking countries of South America are Argentina, Bolivia, Chile, Colombia, Ecuador, Paraguay, Perú, Uruguay, and Venezuela. In addition to mainland countries there are numerous islands in both the Atlantic and Pacific Oceans and the Caribbean Sea. Areas in which other languages are official, and not covered in this book, are Portuguese-speaking Brazil, Dutch-speaking Suriname, French-speaking French Guiana, and English-speaking Guyana.

Archaeologists believe the earliest civilization in South America dates from about 900 BC. Through the millennia many cultures have thrived, among them at least three whose languages and some cultural elements exist today: the Aymara, Guaraní, and Inca (Quechua).

Just as it did in all parts of the western hemisphere, life changed for the peoples of South America in the late fifteenth century. Christopher Columbus made three historic voyages of discovery and exploration, the first in 1492 when he visited Cuba, Hispaniola, and other small islands; the second the following year when he came to Puerto Rico and many more small islands; the third in 1498 when he first set foot on the mainland, thinking he had reached India.

There has been—and continues to be—scholarly discussion concerning the origin of the name America, but traditionally, and with good evidence, the name is credited to Amerigo Vespucci, Italian maritime agent and explorer who worked with Columbus and who later became a Spanish citizen. It is almost certain that after his own explorations of present-day Brazil, it was he who first announced that Columbus's travels had taken him not to the Orient but to a New World, and that there was yet another ocean before the lands of China and Japan and India could be reached.

The first map known to show America is the Martin Waldseemüller 1507 map of the world, a document now in possession of the U. S. Library of Congress. One of the cartographers wrote at the time of the map's creation: "But now these parts [Europe, Asia, and Africa] have been extensively explored and a fourth part has been discovered by Americus Vespuccius. . .I do not see what right any one would have to object to calling this part after Americus, who discovered it and who is a man of intelligence [and so to name it] Amerige, that is the Land of Americus, or America. . ."

Colonization began almost as soon as exploration, starting on the Caribbean Islands. By 1510 the first permanent mainland settlement was in place, Darien in today's southern Panamá, very near Colombia. Other settlements quickly followed, and by 1550 there were Spanish developments throughout the continent—Colombia, Perú, Venezuela, Chile, Ecuador, Bolivia, Paraguay, Ecuador. The enormous mineral riches of the Inca had been discovered—and confiscated. The native peoples had succumbed to the stronger will and tougher weapons of the newcomers. A new race of mestizos was arising.

Spanish customs and religion combined with native customs and religion in the various parts of South America, and new traditions and celebrations, grew in and around the combination.

Argentina

The Land and Its People

Second largest country in South America, eighth largest in the world, most of Argentina is sparsely populated with fewer than forty million people, nearly half of whom live in and around Buenos Aires, the capital city. Three distinct areas comprise Argentina: Gran Chaco in the north, the Pampas in the central part of the country; and Patagonia in the south. The Atlantic Ocean and the Andes Mountains define most of its east and west borders. Adjacent countries are Bolivia, Paraguay, Brazil, Uruguay, and Chile on the eastern side of the Andes. The southern tip of the country is little more than 600 miles from Antarctica.

Although the name Argentina comes from a Latin word for silver, the country is noted more for agriculture and ranching than for its minerals. Gran Chaco is called by some "the last frontier" in South America. It is a rugged, thorny, subtropical land not suitable for agriculture or ranching and quite under-populated. The Pampas on the other hand, broad grassy plains in the heartland of the country, gave rise to the famed *gauchos*, Argentine cowboys who work the large *estancias* (ranches). Not surprisingly, this area is noted for its cattle. Patagonia is a great desert plateau noted for raising sheep. It extends to the Antarctic region of Tierra del Fuego whose capital, Ushuaia, is the southernmost city in the world, though a small town in Chile lays claim to being farther south.

Juan Díaz de Solís was the first, in 1516, to explore the coastline of Argentina. Buenos Aires was settled a few years later, and the cattle industry was established by 1580. There was no question as to Spain's claim to the land of Argentina until 1806 when English forces invaded the country. Within a year the invaders had been expelled, and in 1810 Argentina, along with other Spanish nations in the hemisphere, declared its independence from Spain to become la República Argentina.

The largest groups of indigenous peoples in Argentina were the Tehuelches in Patagonia and the Araucanos in the north. Today's Argentines are mostly mestizos or people of European ancestry, especially Spanish, but there are other large populations who claim Italian, German, or Swiss ancestry. Spanish is the official language, but English, Italian, German, and French are spoken by many, and Quechua is the language among many of the northern natives.

Political life in Argentina has been one of extreme contrasts—between times of peace and times of violence, between conservative and liberal leaders, between civilian and military rule—and its journey toward democracy has been a difficult one. In the mid-twentieth century Juan Perón became the authoritarian leader of the country after a successful coup. He and his wife, Evita, were popular with the working class, but in 1955 another coup usurped their power and they were exiled. Some twenty years later, after Evita's death, Perón was returned to power. He named his new wife, Isabel Martinez, vice president, and when he died in 1974 she became the first woman head of state in the hemisphere. Her term of office was shortlived because in 1976 still another coup occurred, bringing once again military rule and with it inflation and violence.

Early in the twenty-first century new leadership brought about reform that curbed runaway inflation, established a good economy, and moved the country along its road to democracy. Argentina has been a world leader in setting voluntary greenhouse gas targets to fight pollution.

With so vast a country and with many different ethnic groups who bring their own traditions with them, it is not surprising that Christmas customs are varied through the land, reflecting those of their countries of origin.

✳ Christmas Traditions

December marks the beginning of a joyous season. Because Argentina is south of the equator, it is the beginning of summer and the time of preparation for summer vacation and carnival season, as well as for Christmas. Beginning late in November, groups—mostly children—form to sing *los aguinaldos*, songs dedicated to the Christ Child, going from house to house begging for treats in exchange for songs.

The season begins officially with the Feast of the Immaculate Conception on December 8. Often during December weekends friends and work associates meet to celebrate the season in small, intimate groups. It is a long season, ending only with the Feast of Candelaria on February 2.

Early December is the time to bring out *el árbol de Navidad*, often an imitation tree, and to decorate it with lights and ornaments, perhaps with a Santa Claus figure at the top, sometimes with cotton balls to signify snow. Children write letters to request gifts from *Papá Noel*. Excitement grows as the days progress toward the 25th.

This is the time also to build *pesebres* (nativity scenes) in homes and sometimes living crèches, *pesebres vivientes,* in churches. The Baby Jesus is not placed in the crib until Christmas Eve, *la Nochebuena*, the climax of the season. Extended families gather together, everybody bringing food to add to the grand Christmas dinner that usually occurs around 10 o'clock. Fireworks and water balloons fill the air, Chinese lanterns float down the river. On this night in villages near the Bolivian border, *la danza de los cintos* is performed. This is a traditional dance using brightly colored ribbons wound and unwound around a pole, much like the maypole dance. Observers sing *villancicos* during the dance.

Most families go together to *la misa de gallo*. When they return home late into the night, the little ones open the presents left under the tree by *Papá Noel,* and older young people may go out dancing until dawn. Christmas Day and the days following are times for visiting friends and relatives.

In neighborhoods of Buenos Aires there is a New Year's Eve custom of making large doll-like figures of paper and wood. These *muñecos,* sometimes portraying evils of the old year, are filled with fireworks and burned to welcome in the new year.

There are still more gifts in store for the children after *Papá Noel* has come and gone and the new year has begun, for *los Tres Magos,* or *los Tres Reyes,* will arrive on the eve of January 6th, *El día de los Reyes.* The children place their shoes outside their rooms and leave snacks of water and hay for the Kings' camels outside the house. In the morning there are gifts in the shoes, and the visitors have had their refreshment and moved on.

Times for Christmas dinner may be different with different families—some have dinner around 10 p.m., before *la misa;* others go to mass first and have dinner very late into the night. But whenever it occurs, the Christmas dinner is a festive highlight of the celebration. Often the meal is eaten outside in the pleasant summer air. Many different foods are featured, usually with the country's favorite barbecued beef or *lechón,* suckling pig, as the centerpiece. Another favorite is *niños envueltos* (stuffed cabbage rolls, but literally enveloped children). For dessert there are cakes topped with *sidra,* sparkling apple juice often laced with liquour, puddings, *turrones,* candy and nuts, *pan dulce* (sweet bread), and cookies.

Bolivia

The Land and its People

Bolivia, in size about equal to the combined area of Texas and California, is one of only two landlocked countries in South America. Its surrounding neighbors are Perú, Brazil, Paraguay, Argentina, and Chile. The western third of the country, enclosed by Andes mountain ranges, is a high plateau, the Altiplano, with an average altitude of 12,000 feet. Bolivia's capital, La Paz, at an altitude of 11,910 feet is the highest capital city in the world. The northern and eastern two-thirds comprise tropical rain forests and, where Bolivia meets Argentina, the lowlands, known as Gran Chaco, a semi-arid plain.

The population, almost nine million, is estimated to be 85% indigenous or mestizo. Descendents of the ancient Incas, the natives are mostly Quechua-speaking or Aymará-speaking. Though Spanish is the traditional official language, in recent times both Quechua and Aymará have been named official languages as well.

Bolivia's history reaches far back into the ancient world. By about 600 BC the Tiahuanaco empire had been established on the Altiplano and was centered around the famous Lake Titicaca. This civilization flourished until around 1200 AD.

After the collapse of the Tiahuanacans, first the Aymará, then the Quechua became leaders in the region. The Quechua, whom we know as the Inca, quickly absorbed the Aymará and established a vast, rich and powerful, highly advanced empire. It did not, however, have a long life, for in 1532 invading Spanish explorers defeated the Incas and established Spanish rule.

Because of its geography—high mountains and an inland position—Bolivia was not explored as early as Perú, but once the Spaniards discovered its rich supply of silver, the area developed very quickly. First called Upper Perú, Bolivia's first city, Sucre, originally Chuqisaca, later La Plata, then Charcas, was founded in 1538, and in 1544 the world's richest silver mine was discovered and the city of Potosí was established.

The Incas were quickly overrun by the forces of Francisco Pizarro and Diego de Almagro, and the land was under Spanish control until 1825 when it won its independence and was named for the liberator Simón Bolívar.

The silver mining industry gradually faded and finally collapsed, leaving Bolivia in poverty and political unrest. Two wars brought about loss of national territory: the War of the Pacific in 1879-1884 when Bolivia lost to Chile its claim to a small coastal area, and the Chaco War in 1935 when it lost its Chaco territories to Paraguay,

Since its independence from Spain, Bolivia is said to have had 192 governments.

✳ Christmas Traditions

Like most other countries, Bolivia's traditions of Christmas celebration differ between rural and urban settings, between natives and mestizos, and from one geographical region to another. And, like almost all of South America, Bolivia is south of the equator, so Christmas is a summer holiday.

In Cochabamba the *feria Navideña* (Christmas fair) is the year's outstanding event. Vendors bring goods they have worked on all year to *la cancha*, the large open-air market. Their tables are decorated with wreaths and lights, and plastic animals of the *pesebre*. Everything imaginable is for sale.

Flowers and music are very important all over the country. Children begin to gather flowers, especially the *pastora*, similar to the poinsiettia, early in December. Churches get out their silver and gold figures for scenes of the Nativity, and every family gets its Christmas tree and begins to build its *pesebre.* In rural areas there are feasts of thanksgiving and prayers to Mother Earth asking for a good year to come, with a fruitful harvest and no plagues.

In some places a figure of Baby Jesus is placed at the top of a flight of stairs covered in white fabric, surrounded by *la Virgen María* and *San José, los Tres Reyes,* the animals from the manger. Crowds gather round to sing *villancicos* and *tonadas de niño.*

Throughout the country the season is a special time for friends and families to come together, for people to be filled with a spirit of joy and good will. Families gather for *la cena de Nochebuena,* for midnight *brindis* and *abrazos.* Children open their gifts, often at midnight. All go together to *la misa de gallo.* Many families attend *la misa de Navidad* on Christmas morning to ask for a special blessing from the Baby Jesus.

In the old city of Sucre after *la misa de gallo,* a statue of the Baby Jesus is carried in *la procesión del Niño,* through the streets to a place of honor. There, at the foot of the *nacimiento,* to please the Baby, the crowd dances and sings *villancicos* until dawn. Accompanying the merrymakers are native instruments such as *la quena,* a notched, open-ended flute; *la zampoña,* pan pipes; and *el charango,* an instrument with strings stretched across a soundboard traditionally made from the back of an armadillo.

Pan dulce Navideño and rich hot chocolate are stars in Christmas breakfast, *el dulce desayuno.*

Chile

The Land and Its People

A long, narrow ribbon of land extending down half the length of the continent, Chile has a Pacific coastline of nearly 3,000 miles. Its neighbors are Argentina, with which it shares the Andes Mountains, Perú, and Bolivia. In the north is the Atacama Desert, said to be the driest place on earth. Southern Chile includes numerous mountainous islands as well as the Ice Fields of Patagonia, the largest mass of ice in the world outside Greenland and Antarctica, and Cape Horn, the southernmost point in South America, where the Atlantic and Pacific meet. Easter Island and the Juan Fernandez Islands in the eastern Pacific are also Chilean territory.

Along the western side of the Andes, which run the length of Argentina, there are dense concentrations of volcanoes, some 2000 extinct or active. The country is also prone to earthquakes and resultant tidal waves. About half of the Chilean coastline is included in the southeastern section of the Ring of Fire, a zone encircling the Pacific Ocean, the arena for frequent earthquakes and volcanic eruptions.

Approximately one-third of its just over sixteen million inhabitants live in the capital city, Santiago, located near the center of the country.

Fernando Magellan, Portuguese explorer sailing under the flag of Spain, was the first European explorer to visit Chile. In 1520 in an effort to find a channel linking the Atlantic Ocean to the Pacific, Magellan discovered Canal de todos los santos (Channel of all saints) now known as the Straits of Magellan.

By the late 1400s the empire of the Incas included the northern part of Chile, but the native Mapuche, also known as Araucanos, resisted Inca expansion in central and southern Chile. In 1540 Pedro de Valdivia established a Spanish settlement, founding Santiago in 1541. A legend concerning the decisive battle in this area places the patron saint of Spain, San Diego (St. James, also Santo Iago) at the scene. Captured native fighters told the victorious Spaniards that a white man on a white horse, the proverbial image of St. James who is said to have miraculously appeared to aid Spaniards in various battles historically, had suddenly appeared on the battlefield. This so frightened the natives that they dropped their weapons and fled.

Valdivia was killed in 1554 by the Araucanos who continued intermittent attacks on the Spanish settlements into the early nineteenth century. Chile's independence from Spain came in 1818 when an army led by Bernardo O'Higgins defeated the Spanish Royalists and la República de Chile was born. Many theories surround the origin of the name Chile. Perhaps most likely is the indigenous Mapuche word chilli, "where the land ends."

Chile has lived through various dictatorships, military rule, Marxist regime, and parliamentary government.

✳ Christmas Traditions

Christmas celebration in Chile begins with Advent in early December and lasts until the Epiphany, January 6, a day called la *pascua de los negros* in honor of the Three Kings, one of whom they believe came from Africa.

Pascua is a word used throughout Latin America for the religious festivals of Easter, Christmas, Pentecost, and Epiphany. Its plural in Chile usually signifies Christmas, so that *dar las pascuas* is to wish a merry Christmas or a *feliz Navidad*.

School has ended and summer vacation has begun, and children are greatly involved in decorating their houses, setting up *el árbol de pascuas*, and building the *pesebre*. As in other countries, the Christmas season is especially a time for families and friends to come together. Children eagerly await the arrival of *el viejo pascuero* (the old Christmas gentleman) and his reindeer, even though there is no snow this time of year, the reindeer far from their own environment.

Many Chileans keep a novena, the nine days leading up to Christmas Eve. On Christmas Eve some attend *la misa de gallo* at 6:00 and come home to their *cena de Nochebuena*. This festive meal features roast turkey or chicken, *choclo*, and many desserts. At midnight they reflect on the *pesebre* and the meaning of Christmas, often reading the biblical story of the Nativity and singing *villancicos*. Then they pass *brindis* and *abrazos*, and the children open their gifts, some having dedicated their gifts to the Baby Jesus. Others may have their *cena* earlier, then attend *la misa* at the more traditional midnight hour, and come home to have coffee and *pan de pascua*.

El viejo pascuero comes in the night after the children have finally gone to bed, coming in through the chimney or a window, leaving still more gifts for the children to discover on Christmas Day.

Chile has a tradition of much gift-giving—employers to their employees, businesses to their clients, to every person who has done one a favor, to every friend and family member, and many gifts to the children.

Traditions differ somewhat from zone to zone, but everywhere the spirit of the season goes on through the new year and to January 6.

Colombia

The Land and Its People

Colombia enjoys the unique position among South American countries of having a coastline on both the Pacific Ocean and the Caribbean Sea. Panamá is a neighboring country, serving as a separator between the two bodies of water. Venezuela and Brazil border its eastern side and Ecuador and Perú its southern side. A small part of southern Colombia between Perú and Brazil lies south of the equator, and a small neck of land reaches the Amazon River. It is a large country, almost twice the size of Texas.

Cordilleras of the Andes occupy the western half of the country where most of Colombia's approximately forty-four million people live. The eastern half is a low, sparsely populated, tropical plain.

The Chibchas were the predominant linguistic group in pre-Hispanic Colombia; there is evidence they had been there for many hundreds of years. Two principal divisions of the Chibchas were the Muiscas who lived in the highlands around present-day Bogotá, and the Taironas who lived in the Caribbean coastal area around Santa Marta. Today a small population of Kogis, who claim ancestry to the Taironas, live in the Santa Marta area.

Explorers from Spain arrived in the early years of the sixteenth century. In 1510 Alonso de Ojeda established Darien, the first permanent settlement on the mainland of the New World, in an area now known as Panamá, very near present-day Colombia. Fifteen years later Rodrigo de Bastidas founded Santa Marta on the northern coast of Colombia. Seeking an inland route to Perú, Spanish explorers led by Gonzalo Jiménez de Quesada established a settlement in the interior that he called Santa Fé de Bogotá, named for Bacata a name the Chibcha

Indians gave to the area. It became the capital of "the kingdom of New Granada," as its founder called it.

New Granada's independence from Spain was won in 1819, and, led by the great liberator Simón Bolívar, the area known today as Colombia, Panamá, and Venezuela became Gran Colombia, Bolívar's first hope for uniting the Spanish colonies of the New World. This federation was joined by present-day Ecuador in 1822. By 1831, however, the alliance of Gran Colombia had collapsed, and the separate countries of Colombia, Venezuela, and Ecuador emerged. Panamá remained a district of the Republic of Colombia until 1903 when it became an independent republic.

Colombia has struggled with political conflicts among liberals and conservatives, Marxist guerillas, and drug cartels. Its economy is based largely on agricultural products, notably the famous Colombian coffee, but also on oil and minerals.

✷ Christmas Traditions

An outstanding beginning of the Christmas season in Colombia is the celebration of *el día de las velitas*, on December 7, the eve of *el día de la Virgen Inmaculada*. In this great festival of light, also called *el alumbrado*, thousands of candles line the streets, gardens and fences, balconies and rooftops. Elaborate designs are created from arrangements of *farolitos* and candles of all shapes and sizes, and children create forms from the melted wax. This beautiful tradition of thanksgiving is a symbol to colombianos of the path from darkness to the light that guides them toward realization of their highest goals.

In earlier times a custom now forbidden because of the danger of fire was *los globos elevar* (ascension of the balloons). Large lanterns made of light-weight paper were placed over a fire that pushed hot air into them, then lifted them high into the sky.

Another event that occurs at this time, in Medellin, is a tradition that began only in the 1970s but that addresses ancient myths and legends, *el encuentro nacional de mitos y leyendas*. Characters from these stories that come from Spain, Africa, and indigenous sources are represented by floats in a parade through the city streets that are decorated lavishly with wreaths, colored lights, and candles. The city government awards a prize to the street with the most creative *alumbrado navideño*.

An important custom in some areas is *el ropatón* in which people give clothing and shoes, as well as toys for the children, to those most in need.

Community *pesebres* are built in city plazas and in churches, and all over the country people prepare them in their homes, with clay or plastic figures and an empty cradle awaiting *Nochebuena* when the youngest member of the family places the Baby Jesus in it. Children write letters to *el Niño Dios* in which they ask for gifts. These letters are placed in the *pesebre,* from which they soon disappear—taken by *el Niño Dios*, who, they hope, will answer them with gifts on Christmas Eve or Christmas morning.

December 16 begins the *novena de aguinaldos* to honor the Virgin Mary, St. Joseph, the Wise Men, and the Baby Jesus. Throughout the nine days families and friends attend mass in the early mornings and gather in the evenings around the *pesebres* to pray and to sing *villancicos*. Children play *juegos* (games) *de aguinaldo* while they wait for *Nochebuena*. One of these games is *dar y no recibir* (to give and not to receive). In this game one player gives something to another. The receiver has to respond with an *aguinaldo* given back to the donor. The point is to remain watchful so as not to be given anything!

The day of Christmas Eve is a time for families to work together in preparing *natillas* and *buñuelos* that will be among the desserts for *la cena de Navidad*. *Natillas* are made over an outside wood fire. The aroma of the simmering coconut and cinnamon draws many helpers to assist in stirring the mixture in the *paila* (large pot) with a large wooden paddle. Another family tradition from times past but still observed in some places is preparation of *el lechón*, the slow cooking of the pig that will be the main entrée. Other foods usually found in *la cena* include *tamales, potato salad, galletas* (cookies), *manjar blanco* (custard-like pudding), and *hojuelas* (flaky pastry). Dinner on Christmas Eve comes comes late in the evening, after other traditional events.

Pilar Posada recalls the Christmases of her childhood when all the extended family gathered at her grandparents' *finca* (farm, property). During the day on *Nochebuena*, the *mayordomo* (foreman) and all the *campesinos* (country people) had come to the house to receive gifts from the *patrón* (owner) and to exchange Christmas greetings with each other.

After a great display of *pólvora* (fireworks), the family gathered around *el árbol de Navidad* to wait for *Papá Noel*. Excitement built when they began to hear his bell, the sound coming first from one direction, then another as *Papá Noel* tried to keep the children guessing. At last he would burst into the room with his heavy pack that held a present for each person.

When the gifts had been opened and admired, it was time for the more serious part of the evening. They all went into another room where an elaborate *pesebre* had been created early in December. The Holy Family and the manger scene were the highlights, but much else was added: a little waterfall, lakes and rivers, animals, little village houses. They said prayers for the last day of the novena and sang *villancicos*.

On Christmas morning children awakened to find their beds surrounded by gifts brought in response to their letters to *el Niño Dios*.

El día de los santos inocentes comes three days after Christmas and is the cause for a different kind of festive activity, a time for jokes and tricks, *chistes* and *bromas*. People are warned to step carefully and to keep their eyes open because friends are waiting to play tricks on them.

El fin del año, New Year's Eve, is another special day in the celebration of the season. Colombians observe many traditions common to other South American countries, partying with family and friends, with much dancing and singing. Good luck comes with wearing new yellow items of clothing, especially underwear, and from eating twelve grapes and making a wish for each one as the midnight bells toll. The old folk tradition of *la cabañuela,* a way to predict the weather of the coming year, is considered and discussed. According to this method of forecasting the weather, the first twelve days of January will provide a vision of what the whole new year's twelve months will be like; the weather on January 1 describes all of January, on January 2 all of February, on January 3, March, and on through the year.

Large puppets filled with old clothes, straw, and other useless things are built to symbolize the passing of the old to make room for the new. These *muñecos* are placed alongside the roadways for passersby to enjoy before they are burned on New Year's Day.

A January first tradition for many is *el paseo de olla* (stroll of the pot). Once again extended families come together. They travel outside the cities, looking at the *muñecos* and bringing with them huge *ollas* of *sancocho* (Colombian soup) that they will share when they find their picnic place. Sometimes this involves a trip to the beach to lie in the sun and play in the water, especially for those who may have partied too hard the night before.

Another New Year's tradition is *la marranada* when business people invite all their employees to a day of feasting. A pig is killed and cooked outside, and all the meat is eaten—in roast pork, *carne frita* (fried meat), *chicharrones* (crisp fried pork rind), *tripas morcilla* (blood pudding), or in any other form they can think of.

El día de los Reyes Magos, January 6, is a day especially devoted to gifts, another observance of *el paseo de olla,* and visits between godparents and their godchildren. *Padrinazgo,* sponsorship of godparents, is an established, respected institution in Colombia, and godparents are very special in the lives of the children they sponsor.

Ecuador

The Land and Its People

Ecuador is one of South America's smallest countries, in area about the size of the state of Colorado, bounded on the west by the Pacific Ocean, on the north by Colombia, and on the south and east by Perú. It is topographically divided into three distinct regions: la costa, rich coastal plains; la sierra, highlands with year-round snow-covered mountains; and el oriente, the tropical forest on the east slope of the Andes.

Most of Ecuador is below the equator, for which the country is named. Its seasons are defined more by rainfall than by temperature: January through April is the rainy season, May through December drier and cooler.

Home to thousands of species of flora and fauna in its rainforests, mountains, and deserts, Ecuador is one of the most ecologically diverse countries in the world. The Galapagos Islands, about 600 miles from mainland Ecuador, was the source for Charles Darwin's earliest studies of his theory of evolution and the principle of natural selection.

Hunters and gatherers established settlements on the southern coast and in the central highlands of present-day Ecuador thousands of years ago. Evidence suggests the Valdivia culture, one of the oldest known cultures in the world, existed along the coast as early as 3500 BC. The area was populated by Valdivias and other groups, including the Canari, the Quitu, and the Caras, long before the Incas arrived and assumed leadership in the middle of the fifteenth century.

Francisco Pizarro and 180 armed men landed in present day Ecuador in 1532, handily overcoming the Incas, and beginning a 300-year reign of Spanish governors. The first Spanish settlement was established in 1534 at

Quito, an important Inca town and today the capital of the country.

Ecuador was part of the Viceroyalty of Perú until 1740 when it was transferred to the Viceroyalty of New Granada. After liberator Simón Bolívar led a successful rebellion in 1822, Ecuador, Venezuela, and Colombia became Gran Colombia. Ecuador seceded from this union in 1830 and became la República de la Ecuador.

Military dictators were in charge of Ecuador's government for nearly a century and a half, but free elections have been held since 1979.

✳ Christmas Traditions

Early in December Ecuadorian children write letters to *el Niño Dios,* or *Papá Noel.* Christmas preparations begin in every home with a Christmas tree, often an artificial tree, and building sometimes elaborate *pesebres* with figures of porcelain or wood.

La novena del Niño begins December 16, and each night until Christmas Eve friends gather together to pray to *el Niño* and sing *villancicos* before the *pesebres.*

For *la Navidad de los pobres* (Christmas of the poor people), rural workers dressed in their finest clothes, come to the cities or to the ranches of their *patrones* (owners, overseers) bringing gifts of produce and crafts, and in return asking for *la Navidad,* gifts from their employers. Gifts are exchanged, the children recite poems to the Baby Jesus and pray for a blessing on their animals and all people. The fiesta ends with a grand dinner for the workers and their families.

In times past *la cena de Nochebuena* was traditionally held at midnight, but it is generally earlier than that now so that all can attend *la misa de gallo* at midnight. In some homes children open their presents on Christmas Eve, but it is more common for them to wait until Christmas morning to see what *el Niño Dios* has left at the foot of their beds.

An ancient and colorful custom in Cuenca is *el pase del Niño viajero* (the parade of the wandering Child), a tradition with mixed symbolism from the mestizo and Indian cultures. Its origin is unknown, but it undoubtedly began in Spanish colonial days. *El Niño* is a wooden image made in 1823. It was taken in the 1960s by a priest on his journey to holy places, finally being blessed by the Pope. Since then it has been known as the wandering child, *el Niño viajero.*

El pase winds through the streets of Cuenca, led by a star representing the Star of Bethlehem, followed by the Holy Family, *el Niño viajero* carried on a platform by priests of the church, angels, shepherds, the Three Kings, gypsies, cowboys, elaborate floats depicting biblical scenes, and hundreds of children dressed in their traditional Andean clothes.

Other *pasadas* for the Baby Jesus exist, from the first Sunday of Advent until Easter, but this is the *gran pasada* and is unequalled in splendor and color by any other event in Cuenca.

There is a statue of the Christ Child in every neighborhood in Saraguro. In *el pase del Niño,* people join in procession at the church to carry the statue to a specially chosen house, the home of the "godparent" to the image. Preceded by musicians, the procession includes dancers dressed as bears, devils, and other fierce creatures whose duty is to protect the Christ Child. A grand feast ends this ceremony.

Immediately after Christmas plans get underway for *la fiesta del año viejo,* the feast of the old year. Puppets and large dolls to represent gloom and unhappiness of the year, political or worldly situations, are made of sawdust and paper. The puppets are judged, and the makers of the winner receive a trophy and a gift of money.

The puppets are burned at midnight amidst fireworks and general revelry to signify the passing of the old year with all its troubles and the coming of the new, full of hope. In some places children assume the role of the "widow" of *el año viejo* and beg coins, *"la caridad,"* charity, since their "husband" has been burned in the observance.

Paraguay

The Land and Its People

Paraguay, about the size of California, is landlocked in the middle of South America. The Paraguay River defines its border with Brazil and partially with Argentina; Bolivia is a third bordering country. The Paraguay River is a major South American waterway, navigable for a distance second only to the navigable length of the Amazon. The world's largest hydroelectric power plant is on the Brazil/Paraguay border, and the largest wetland system in the world, El Gran Pantanal, comprises 50,000 acres in Paraguay, Brazil, and Bolivia.

The river flows through the center of Paraguay, dividing the terrain into two distinctly different environments. The eastern region is an area of grassy slopes and wooded hills inclining toward the river. The chaco region in the west is covered with marshes, swamps, dense forests and jungles, including its section of the Pantanal. The river eventually joins the Paraná River which in turn is part of the great río de la Plata system.

The population of Paraguay is extremely homogeneous, some 95 percent of its population of Spanish and Guaraní descent. Both Spanish and Guaraní are official languages, and most of the people are fluent in both. The great majority of the six and a half million Paraguayans live in the eastern region near the capital city of Asunción.

The name of the country is derived from a Guaraní word, pararaguay, meaning "from a great river.

In 1516 an ill-fated expedition led by Juan Díaz de Solís sailed up the Paraná River in search of a shorter passage to the Pacific which had been discovered by Balboa three years before, but the mission was cut short by the assassination of Díaz de Solís. His men named the river rio de Solís in his honor and hastily made their retreat.

En route back to Spain, one of their ships was wrecked near the Brazilian coast. A survivor, Aleixo García, made plans to continue the aborted exploration, and eight years later, in 1524, he led an expedition back into the area. García was able to make friends with the Guaraní and enlisted two thousand of these natives to accompany him overland in his westward journey; thus he was the first European to cross the chaco and to break into the outer lines of the Incan defense.

García too was killed on his journey but not before he had discovered rich treasures of silver. Word spread, and in 1526 an Italian sailing for Spain, Sebastian Cabot, attempted to duplicate García's journey to find a shorter route to the Orient. He did not find the route he sought, but he traded successfully with the Guaraní, renamed the river el río del plato, and was able to take a number of silver objects back to King Charles V of Spain in 1530.

The king immediately appointed Don Pedro de Mendoza to establish a settlement in what is now Paraguay. Mendoza was not successful, but his successor, Juan de Salazar de Espinosa, established a colony on the church feast day of the Assumption, August 15, 1537. He called it Asunción.

This settlement quickly became the base of operations for colonization and for all the Spanish holdings in southern South America.

In 1607 a unique social experiment called *reducciones* was begun by Jesuit missionaries who had been sent to convert the Guaraní. This plan called for small autonomous, self-sustaining communities of the native population. It freed them from the near-slavery conditions they had been placed in, and it provided for protection and security. Colonists and slave traders were strongly opposed to the system, but it existed for a century and a half. Finally, in 1767, the opponents convinced Charles III of Spain to expel the Jesuits and dissolve the *reducciones*.

Like other nations in South America Paraguay declared its independence from Spain in the early 1800s. For the nineteenth and most of the twentieth centuries the country lived in political instability, under authoritarian or military rule.

❊ Christmas Traditions

Paraguayans are a deeply religious people, and their celebration of Christmas reflects that. There are gifts for young children, but the emphasis of the season is on the warmth and love of family and friends rather than on gifts.

The towns and villages begin early in December to decorate with lights and flowers. Every home builds its own *pesebre*, mostly of branches, plants, fruits, and other natural items. Each *pesebre* prominently displays the *cocotero*, fragrant flower of the coconut palm.

La fiesta de la patrona on December 8, in honor of the Virgin Mary, begins *la Navidad en familia*, and the next weeks are spent in preparation for *Nochebuena*.

Children singing *villancicos* go from house to house to visit and pray before the *pesebres* in remembrance of the shepherds' visit to the Baby Jesus. These visits can occur throughout December, but they are very special on Christmas Eve and Christmas morning. The children are rewarded with sweets and delicacies.

Christmas Eve dinner may come either before or after *la misa de gallo*. It traditionally features roast pork or chicken, *clerico*, a sweet wine punch, and *sopa paraguaysa*, a cheesy cornbread.

Papá Noel may come before Christmas morning to leave a few presents in the children's shoes. More often the time for presents is January 5 when the Three Kings pass through, taking the grass and water the children have prepared for them and their camels and leaving gifts in their shoes. In some places *el Señor de la bolsa* who, legend says, carried small children in his bag, has begun to replace *Papá Noel*, who now, instead of carrying children in his bag, carries gifts for the children.

Perú

The Land and Its People

Perú is a large South American country, about twice the size of Texas, slightly smaller than Alaska. Its western border is the Pacific coastline; its adjoining neighbors are Brazil, Bolivia, Chile, Ecuador, and Colombia. It comprises three distinct areas, the costa, the sierra, and the selva.

The western costa is partly desert and partly arid river valleys of irrigated agricultural land. The Sierra, the Andes, is made up of two long ranges, the cordillera occidental and the cordillera oriental, with peaks in both over 20,000 feet. In the southern part of the cordilleras are many volcanoes and lakes. These ranges are covered by rivers that make up the headwaters of the Amazon River. Lake Titicaca, highest navigable lake in the world at more than 12,500 feet above sea level, lies in the Andes on the border between Perú and Bolivia. The ancient village below the famous peak Machu Picchu lies in these mountains where it remained undiscovered by the outside world until the twentieth century.

The sierra is populated mostly with descendents from the Incas and other indigenous groups. The selva is a dense tropical rain forest, the enormous Amazon jungle shared with Brazil, very sparsely populated.

Perú has about 28,000,000 residents, some eight million living in the capital, Lima, which was established in 1537. The name Perú is most likely from a corruption of a village name, biruquete, meaning granary.

Often called the cradle of the Incas, Perú was home to numerous other tribes and civilizations before the Inca came on the scene. There is some evidence that hunters and gatherers populated the land twenty thousand years ago, and many diverse groups, among them Chavín, Sechin, Wari, Chanka, lived in various degrees of organized society.

In spite of their being the greatest pre-Columbian civilization on the continent, the height of the Incas' power was to last just under a hundred years, from 1438 until the Spaniards came in 1532. From the twelfth to the early fifteenth centuries they lived in a small valley near Cuzco, assimilating small tribes and building their great society. The Incas defeated the Chankas in a decisive battle in 1438. Legend says the boulders of the battlefield turned into Incan warriors that helped defeat the enemy.

The Inca set about expanding their kingdom through much of South America, establishing Tahuantinsuyo, the "Four United Regions." They created a system of roads, the Inca Trail, that expedited travel and communication among all their peoples. They had *chasquis*, message carriers, who relayed information throughout the empire. The Incas believed that harmony and balance of man, nature, and the gods was essential to life.

Francisco Pizarro had been with Nuñez de Balboa in Panamá when Balboa discovered the Pacific Ocean in 1513. Within a short time Pizarro was to hear of vast riches of silver in lands to the south, and in 1530 he set sail for Perú to claim the land and its treasure for Charles V of Spain.

The Incas were well organized and they were fierce warriors, but their weapons of clubs and stones were no match for the armor-wearing, mounted Spaniards with their firearms, and the Inca Empire collapsed in 1532.

Very quickly Lima was recognized as the central point of western South America, the seat of expansionist activities. The years of Spanish colonialism were years of exploitation, of resources and of the natives, in Perú. In 1821 peruanos declared their independence from Spain, though it was not until 1824 that Perú was declared a republic.

Centuries of instability with military or authoritarian rule followed, as well as wars with neighboring countries concerning border disputes during the nineteenth and twentieth centuries. Social and economic reforms were introduced in the late twentieth century.

✳ Christmas Traditions

Preparations start in early December with lights and decorations, Christmas trees and *pesebres* in shops and homes and churches. Many peruanos expand their *pesebres* from the Holy Family to include Noah's Ark, llamas made of gold and silver, Abraham's sacrifice, and familiar figures such as the *tamal* seller, the baker, the jasmine seller, and more. *The novena de aguinaldo* begins on December 16. Business owners often give their employees *canastas navideñas* (Christmas baskets) filled with champagne, *panetón* (sweet fruit bread), and various other things for Christmas dinner preparation.

In the busy shopping days before Christmas *campesinos* from deep in the mountains come to town bringing their crafts and produce. In Cusco, ancient capital of the Incas, a *feria santurantikuy*, a market for selling figures of saints, is held in the public square. Shop owners and employers host *chocolotadas* where a festive fruited Italian bread, *panetón*, is served along with hot chocolate and a toy for the children.

The Christmas tree is not so prominent in Perú, but most families construct a *nacimiento*. On Christmas Eve masked musicians and groups of children stroll through the streets singing and dancing. They go from house to house visiting each family's *nacimiento*. In some places children dressed as *los pastores* in the colorful clothes of their region sing in the churches. These *pastorcitos* may go from house to house in the days following Christmas, accompanied by city officials who judge which family *nacimiento* is the best.

Families and friends gather on *la Nochebuena*, first to attend *la misa de gallo*. Here their *Niño Manuelito* figure is blessed, then taken home where the head of the household places it in the crib. Often fireworks, a champagne toast, and *abrazos* and wishes of *feliz Navidad* occur around midnight. The traditional Christmas meal featuring roast turkey or pork, tamales, apple sauce, more *panetón,* and a Peruvian brandy, *pisco*, follows. Sometimes gifts are opened after the meal, making for a very late bedtime.

The customs of wecoming the new year include eating twelve grapes, each accompanied by a wish for the coming year. Yellow booths are set up in the streets, yellow being the color of optimism and good fortune. Many gifts of yellow apparel or yellow miniatures are exchanged, all covered in yellow confetti.

In parts of Perú New Year's Day also sees the *entrega de varas* in which city officials come together to pass a wooden scepter from the outgoing to the incoming mayors, a celebration sealed in good humor with *chichi* (corn whiskey) and *llonque* (sugarcane ale).

In the Indian pueblo of San Pablo, the Three Kings are not known by the familiar names of *Melchor, Gaspar,* and *Baltasar* but instead they are *Inkarri*, Inca King, *Mistirri*, Mestizo King, and *Negrorri*, Negro King, and they arrive not on camels but in a horse-drawn cart.

Uruguay

The Land and Its People

Smallest of all the Spanish-speaking countries in South America (Suriname, Dutch-speaking, is smaller), Uruguay is about the size of Oklahoma. It lies between Brazil and Argentina. One hundred twenty miles of Atlantic coastline form its eastern border, and the río de la Plata and the río Uruguay comprise its western border. Southern Uruguay consists of low rolling plains; northern Uruguay is a low plateau broken by broad valleys. The coastal grasslands are ideal for raising cattle and sheep.

The proper name of the country is the Oriental Republic of Uruguay, oriental because it is east of the Uruguay River. Uruguay is a Guaraní word meaning river of shell fish or river of the uru birds.

Juan de Solís visited Uruguay in 1516, but the unfriendly native Charruas and the lack of silver and gold riches discouraged extensive Spanish settlement during the sixteenth and earliest years of the seventeenth centuries. Jesuit and Franciscan missionaries landed in 1624, and settlement began. Portugal actually played the most important role in Uruguay's early settlement, founding Colonia del Sacramento in 1680.

The capital, Montevideo, was founded in 1726, and Uruguay became part of the Spanish region of La Plata, with headquarters in Buenos Aires, Argentina. Both Buenos Aires and Montevideo were captured in a British invasion in 1806, but the occupation was short-lived, and the invaders were forced out in 1807.

Led by its national hero, José Gervasio Artigas, Uruguay declared its independence from Argentina in 1815, but it was attacked by the Portuguese soon after, and in 1821 it was made a part of Brazil. It became the Oriental Republic of Uruguay in 1828.

Another struggle, late in the nineteenth century, was the War of the Triple Alliance in which Uruguay joined with Brazil and Argentina to defeat Paraguay.

A tradition as strong in Uruguay as in Argentina is the *gaucho* culture. *Gauchos* were early cowboys, mestizos, who herded sheep and cattle in the *pampas* (plains) and often worked in contraband activities. Later they worked as hands on the ranches and participated in the militia during the struggle for independence. It is said that the spirit of the Charrua lives in today's *gauchos*.

Three and a third million people live in this small country, about half of them in Montevideo. Very few—no more than six per cent—are descendants of the native Charrua Indians. Even fewer—about four per cent—are descendants of Africans who were brought to the country as slaves. The origin of ninety per cent is European, mostly Spanish and Italian.

Uruguay is noted for its beef and wool exports. It is proud of its ninety-nine per cent literacy rate.

✳ Christmas Traditions

Uruguay may have a larger percentage of European immigrant infusion than any other South American country; this would cause it naturally to have great diversity of cultures, including the ways in which its people celebrate Christmas and other holidays. Two elements, though, cut through all layers of Uruguayan culture, the emphasis on gatherings of extended family and the abundance of great food.

Besides Christmas Day itself, three days are of special significance: Christmas Eve, New Year's Eve, and the Day of the Kings. Everybody comes together on Christmas Eve—grandparents, uncles and aunts, cousins, friends–to celebrate *la víspera de Navidad, la Nochebuena*. When all are gathered, they begin the *picadita*, a grand display of "starters," cold cuts, cheeses, small pieces of grilled meats, whisky and wine, juices and soft drinks.

Some go to church before dinner. At midnight, after many *abrazos* and *brindis* with *sidra*, a drink that combines sugar and sweet cider with many varieties of fruit such as apples, oranges, pears, bananas, melon, cherries, grapes, pineapple, everybody goes outside to witness the many fireworks and explosives. Then comes *la cena de Navidad,* usually featuring grilled lamb or pork, sometimes baked chicken or turkey. Traditional desserts include candies and nuts, and *pan dulce de Navidad* which is served with a glass of cider or even champagne. Almost always this dinner occurs on the patio in *al aire libre* (the open air), since the summer provides excellent weather. From there the younger members of the group leave to be part of the *bailes de Navidad* and the older ones go back to the table, perhaps to organize another *picadita* from the leftovers!

Children may open their gifts after midnight. They believe that to open them before midnight will make the toys turn to ashes.

La víspera de año nuevo, el fin del año, is celebrated in much the same way as *Nochebuena:* families gather together, toast and embrace each other, and share wishes for a happy new year. Fireworks are everywhere, and the night seems made for having fun.

The third day of note is *el día de Reyes,* also called *el día de los niños.* On its eve the children leave their shoes, along with water and straw for the camels, under the Christmas tree; they wake the next morning to find gifts left by the Kings.

Venezuela

The Land and Its People

Venezuela, about twice the size of California, makes up most of South America's northern coast on the Caribbean Sea. Its immediate neighbors are Colombia on the west, English-speaking Guyana on the east, and Portuguese-speaking Brazil on the south.

The land of Venezuela has some of nearly everything—an extension of the Andes Mountains, a segment of the Amazon Jungle, sierras and valleys, plains and lowlands, highlands filled with *tepuis* which are mesa-like, flat-topped mountains with sheer cliffs from one of which Auyantepui (Angel Falls) the highest waterfall in the world drops. South America's third largest river system, after the Amazon and rio de la Plata, is Venezuela's rio Orinoco and its tributaries.

The population is nearly twenty-six million, mostly mestizo, Indian/European/African, with sizable minority groups of Caucasian, Black, and a few native Indians. The great majority of Venezuelans live in cities and towns. Officially this country is the Bolivarian Republic of Venezuela. The reference to the Great Liberator, Simón Bolívar, is obvious. The origin of the word Venezuela is thought to have come from explorer Alonso de Ojeda in 1499, who saw native villages built on stilts over the water. He was reminded of Venice, Italy, and so named the area Veneziela. Christopher Columbus, whose first steps on the mainland of South America were in today's Venezuela, called it isla de gracia, Isle of Grace.

Archaeological evidence suggests that Venezuela was inhabited about 16,000 years ago by nomadic peoples. By the end of the fifteenth century, when European explorers first appeared, the largest native groups were the Arawak, Carib, and Chibcha.

Columbus was the first of the Europeans to visit Venezuela, arriving in 1498 on his third voyage to the western hemisphere. As he explored the río Orinoco delta, he realized his discovery was not just a set of islands but was indeed a larger landmass; he maintained until his death the belief that he had reached the continent of Asia.

The Spanish were in no hurry to colonize the area, probably because they saw little in the way of tangible riches, and they had no idea of the value of the vast quantities of oil that would be exploited centuries later. In 1528 a German banking company became interested in the area and obtained a permit for exploratory and colonization rights, but when no precious metals were discovered, they surrendered their permit in 1556. Caracas, the capital city of Venezuela, was founded in 1567.

About two centuries later, in 1783, Simón Bolívar was born in Caracas. Known not only in Venezuela but also in other South American countries as the Great Liberator, Bolívar led movements for independence from Spain all across the continent. Venezuela's successful independence was declared in 1821. It was Bolívar's dream to merge Venezuela, Colombia, Ecuador, and Panamá into one large republic, Gran Colombia. This union lasted from 1821 until 1830 at which time Venezuela withdrew and became a republic in its own right. In 1999 its full name became the Bolivarian Republic of Venezuela.

The country has survived centuries of military rule, dictatorships, and political instability. It has held democratic elections since 1958.

✳ Christmas Traditions

Music has its place in Christmas celebrations all over the world, but perhaps its position of prime importance in Venezuela is unique even among South American countries.

In addition to *villancicos* and *aguinaldos*, as well as *parrandas*, an offshoot of *aguinaldos*, genres common to all Spanish-speaking areas, Venezuela has another form more particularly its own, the *gaita*. With strong roots in Africa, it was at first purely a protest song. Later one segment of the style, *la gaita zuliana*, turned to themes related to Christmas. In late summer and early fall school groups and others begin to form *gaita* groups; soon rehearsals are underway for *gaita* contests, and *gaitas* are heard on every radio station, in bars and restaurants, and throughout the communities.

By mid-November the sights and sounds of Christmas are everywhere, lights and decorations inside and out, in shops and homes. *Gaiteros* are now joined by *aguinalderos* and *parranderos* who go from house to house singing and praying before the *nacimiento* or the more elaborate *pesebre*. Always their songs are rewarded with sweets or small gifts.

As soon as the first signs of Christmas are in the streets, *los cochinitos de aguinaldo* appear everywhere. These are small plastic pigs placed in strategic places for people to fill with coins, *aguinaldos* for the poor.

December 16 marks the beginning of school holidays, which will last until February 2, as well as the beginning of *las misas de aguinaldo*, the nine daily early morning masses representing the journey to Bethlehem, and leading to *Nochebuena*. It is the custom in Caracas for *patinadores*, roller skaters, to skate every morning to mass. Children at bedtime tie a string around their big toe, then hang the other end of the string out the window for *patinadores* to give it a yank as they skate by. *Los patinadores* gather in front of the church after the early morning *misas de aguinaldos* where vendors are waiting to sell them hot chocolate, *empanadas*, and sweet bread.

At home *el pino de Navidad* is decorated. Throughout the month business owners host their employees, or groups of working friends meet together for *cenas navideñas* consisting of *hallaca* (Venezuelan tamales) and Christmas cheer. In some places on December 21 family members gather for each person to write twenty-one wishes, seven for himself, seven for his family, seven for the world. The papers are then placed in a special place to be brought out again and read next December 21. Fireworks and music are everywhere.

Different traditions exist in various parts of the country; for example in some places there is *la danza de los pastores* in which townspeople gather in front of the church after the Christmas Eve mass to become the shepherds searching for *el Niño Dios*. The angel Gabriel appears to guide them, usually to la Plaza Bolívar, where they dance before the *pesebre*.

At last, *Nochebuena!* Like family observances everywhere, the Venezuelan celebration is a time of coming together to attend *la misa de gallo*, then at home for *el plato navideño* which always features *hallacas*. Also included traditionally are *pan de jamón*, black cake, and various salads and sweets. At midnight the youngest child places the image of the *Niño Dios* in the crèche. Toasts and hugs are shared, and children are allowed to open their presents.

Christmas Day is a time for rest and reflection and perhaps a time to plan for the special events coming in the next few days.

December 28, the Day of the Innocents, is a day of fun and practical jokes for venozolanos, *el dia de locos y locainos* (the crazies). On this day *el jefe de los locos* takes charge of the neighborhoods and villages. Roles are reversed—men as women, women as men; old as young, young as old. There are also a *fiesta de mono* in which the principal character is a monkey, and *el gobierno de las mujeres* where women assume governmental duties and men take care of the households.

In *la parradura del Niño* the image of the Baby Jesus is taken from the crib, placed on a large scarf carried by four people and, joined by others singing *aguinaldos*, paraded from house to house where they all pray before the *nacimientos*.

In other places there are reenactments of the Child Jesus lost then found in the temple. Songs and prayers accompany the procession as images are carried through the village streets. This observance, called *robo y búsqueda*, occurs frequently between December 31 and February 2, the official closing date of the holiday season.

Yellow clothing, especially underwear, is the order of the day for New Year's Eve. This, often presented as a gift, is a sure way to attract good luck in the new year. To eat twelve grapes, making a wish with each one, also brings good luck; to walk outside with a packed suitcase promises a year of travel. The old year and its evils are symbolically burned in a specially prepared puppet figure. At the tolling of the midnight bells there are toasts and hugs and more fireworks, then the holiday supper which is almost as festive as *el plato navideño*.

On January 6 children hurry to see if the straw they left the night before has been replaced with gifts. They are especially thrilled if they find a black smudge on their face, for that tells them Baltazar, the king from Ethiopia, has kissed them.

Central America

Joining North America at Mexico's southern border and South America at a small strip of Colombia's eastern Pacific coast, Central America binds the two continents into the western hemisphere, the Americas. Rimmed on the west by the Pacific Ocean and on the east by the Gulf of Mexico and the Caribbean Sea, this is a geographically active land with numerous volcanic eruptions, earthquakes, and hurricanes.

The six Spanish-speaking countries making up Central America are Costa Rica, El Salvador, Guatemala, Honduras, Nicaragua, and Panamá. A seventh is English-speaking Belize. Some forty million people live in the seven countries.

The principal indigenous peoples at the time of the conquest were the Maya. They had migrated south from their earlier ancestral lands in Mexico, and by about 250 AD they were well established in a highly developed civilization in present-day Guatemala, Honduras, El Salvador, and Belize. They had developed a complex calendar and an elaborate form of hieroglyphics as well as exceptional examples of ceremonial architecture in the form of pyramids and observatories. They were weavers and potters and skilled agriculturists.

The Maya were by no means the only people indigenous to the mountains and jungles of Central America, for there were also Nahua, Lencas, Pipils, and various other groups of Aztec or Inca extraction.

Spain began its conquest of Central America in the 1520s. As in other areas of settlement, its more sophisticated weapons and its desire for conquest and riches soon overran the natives' simple tools and fierce defense of their homeland. They were forced into slave labor conditions that, along with disease and continued battle, destroyed great numbers of them, yet even today the Maya retain many elements of their culture, their clothing styles, their arts, their language.

In 1540 Spain established the Captaincy General of Guatemala that covered almost the whole of Central America. This was the law of the land until 1821 when the Mexican War of Independence drove the governing officials in the New World back to Spain. A representative democracy followed, consisting of Guatemala, Honduras, El Salvador, Nicaragua, and Costa Rica, with its capital at Guatemala City. This union lasted from 1823 to 1838 before it dissolved into individual republics.

Panamá became a department of Colombia, and this important gateway between Atlantic and Pacific found its way to independence in the early twentieth century.

Costa Rica

The Land and Its People

Costa Rica is a small country, about the size of Vermont and New Hampshire together, between Nicaragua on the north and Panamá on the south. It has an ocean on either side, the Pacific on the west and the Caribbean Sea on the east. Costa Rica is especially noted for its enormous variety of plant and animal life. The temperature seems to be always right, neither too hot nor too cold. It has north-to-south mountain ranges and many large rivers. The country has about four-and-a-half million inhabitants, most of whom are of Spanish descent or mestizos of Spanish and Indian ancestry, but there are also significant numbers of people from other European backgrounds, as well as a small percent of Afro-Costa Ricans who emigrated from Jamaica. The most southern point reached by Nahuatl culture was Costa Rica

The capital is San José; the official language is Spanish, but English and various dialects are also commonly spoken.

When Columbus on his last voyage to the New World in 1502 came near the shore of what is now Costa Rica, natives wearing gold pendants rowed out to meet him. This inspired the name Costa Rica, rich coast, and created immediate interest in the land. The natives gave Columbus gold and he returned to Spain with reports of a plentiful supply. Later when the Spaniards began to explore the land, they were disappointed to discover there were no rich lodes of silver and gold, and they concentrated their explorations on lands to the north and south of Costa Rica. It was not until 1562 that a settlement under Governor Juan Vásquez de Coronado was established in Costa Rica. The governor was a relative of Francisco Vásquez de Coronado, sixteenth-century explorer of the American Southwest.

Development of Costa Rica continued slowly as exports of wheat, coffee, and tobacco began to improve its economic condition. In 1821 Costa Rica achieved independence from Spain, along with others of the Spanish colonies in America. Two years later it became a member of the confederation of Central American states. It has been a democratic republic since 1838.

You will hear Costa Ricans refer to themselves as *ticos*, a term which probably came from a saying that arose during Spanish colonial times, "We are all *hermaniticos*, little brothers."

✳ Christmas Traditions

Celebration of *las Navidades* starts in early December when Costa Ricans begin to decorate their homes and businesses with colored lights, ribbons and flowers—especially wild orchids, cypress leaves, and red coffee berries. Every home creates a Nativity scene, a *portal* or *pasito*. These are elaborate representations, sometimes filling the whole living room of a home with small houses, shepherds, angels, sheep, and other animals. Contests are held to choose the best *pasito*.

Aguinaldos, also called *bonos Navideños*, equivalent to one month's salary, are given to workers, and a special Christmas lottery is held, giving prize money to some lucky winners. The houses are swept from *cabo* to *rabo*, head to foot, to clear out the bad luck of the past year and to open a path for the new year to enter with its good luck. Adding extra energy to the observance of this long holiday is the fact that Christmas vacation is also the beginning of summer vacation for the schools which remain closed until March.

Posadas begins on December 16, when to the beat of accompanying drummers, figures of Mary and Joseph are carried through the streets to a chosen house. Each night *villancicos* asking for lodging are sung. The procession is invited into the home for punch, *tamales*, dancing, and more singing. The figures remain in this house until the next night when the procedure is repeated at another house. On the night of *la Nochebuena* at the last house chosen, the Christ Child is added to the *pasito*, and there is the biggest party of all. At the end of the merry-making, everyone goes to la *misa de gallo*, and finally all gather in their homes for *la cena de Nochebuena* which always features *tamales*, *empanadas*, and various other traditional dishes. After supper children put out their shoes for *el Niño Dios* to fill with presents.

On the day after Christmas a great parade of horses and hand-painted oxcarts fills the streets honoring a tradition popular since colonial times. Everyone turns out to see *el tope*, in which individual riders show off their horsemanship and fancy clothes, dance ensembles perform, and Miss *Tica Linda*, queen of *el tope*, leads the parade.

Las corridas de toro, is a sort of rodeo, also a holdover from earlier days. This is Costa Rica's own version of bullfights in which the bulls are never wounded. Many young men rush into the arena together, running, shouting, making all kinds of noise, surprising the bull and provoking him to attack. This activity is exciting to all though it is dangerous and sometimes causes injury to those in the arena, but it persists as a symbolic act designed to get rid of the old year's frustrations.

On January 6 family and friends gather to pray the rosary, to give thanks for the gifts received at Christmas, to put away until next year the *pasito*, and to pray for prosperity in the new year. February 2 brings candelero, a feast day observed forty days after Christmas in a candle-bearing procession around the church.

El Salvador

The Land and Its People

The Republic of El Salvador, smallest of the Central American countries, about the size of Massachusetts, is the only one without an Atlantic coastline. Its bordering neighbors are Guatemala on the west and Honduras on the north and east, with the Pacific Ocean on the south. El Salvador's land is divided by mountains into three regions: the southern coastal belt, the central valleys and plateaus, and the northern mountains. Its population is between six and seven million, most of whom are mestizos. Spanish is its official language, but English and Nahuatl are also spoken.

Archaeological evidence found in the ruins of Tazumal and San Andrés indicates that the area of present-day El Salvador had already been inhabited many hundreds of years by the middle of the eleventh century when the Pipil entered the region. A sub-group of the nomadic Nahua, the Pipil were an agricultural people who fiercely resisted the Spanish incursion into their land, Cuscatlán, meaning the land of precious things. The first attempt at subjugation failed in 1524 when Pedro de Alvarado was forced to retreat, though his forces returned the following year and were successful in overcoming the natives. Alvarado's cousin, Diego de Alvarado, established the capital, San Salvador, in 1525.

In 1821, after an earlier unsuccessful attempt at rebellion, El Salvador joined the rest of Central America in declaring its independence from Spain. Other countries joined with Mexico in 1822, but El Salvador resisted, insisting instead on autonomy. In 1823 a revolution in Mexico led to the decision that Central America should be free from Mexican control, and the United Provinces of Central America was formed. In 1838 El Salvador became an independent state. For the next hundred and fifty years revolutions, military coups, dictatorships, and civil wars were the lot of Salvadorans. Since 1992 El Salvador has been a democratic republic.

✷ Christmas Traditions

Decoration of homes begins early in December, always with a tree included under which the *pesebre* is placed. Reindeer made of hay and vines are also popular decorations in spite of the fact that El Salvador is a semi-tropical country, far from the snowy lands of the reindeer. By mid-month there are frequent displays of fireworks, and on *la Nochebuena* and New Year's Eve, loud explosions are heard everywhere as the sky is lit up with *estrellitas, silbadores,* and *morteros* (sparklers), and very large, whistling, window-shaking firecrackers.

Workers are let off from their jobs around noon on Christmas Eve after receiving their Christmas bonuses. A longstanding tradition is that everyone has new, festive Christmas clothes elaborately decorated with lace and sequins. All dress up and gather together with family and friends in the early evening to watch the yearly *pastorelas*, dramas of the shepherds and the angels, and *posadas*, reenactments of Mary and Joseph's search for lodging. These dramas are replete with elaborate costumes, shepherds' staves, bells, and drums. In some villages there remains the custom of performing the *danza de las cintas*, Dance of the Ribbons, winding and unwinding colorful ribbons around a pole while singing *villancicos*.

La misa de gallo, beginning at midnight, figures prominently in Salvadorans' Christmas observance, with *la cena* being served either late in the evening or, more commonly, after mass. Traditional foods for this festive supper include *pupusas* (turnovers), *tamales*, as well as *galletas* and many other desserts. Although the *pesebres* are set up long before Christmas Eve, it is the custom for the crib to remain empty until just after midnight when the figure of the Baby Jesus is laid in its place.

After mass and supper young people go out to private parties or to the beach while children go to bed to await the visit of *Papa Noë*, and adults remain to visit with each other and to await the partygoers' return in the early morning hours. Finally around 5:00 a.m. all retire for what is left of the night.

Guatemala

The Land and Its People

The Republic of Guatemala, about the size of Tennessee, is in the middle of Central America, its borders on the Caribbean Sea lying between Honduras and Belize, and on the Pacific Ocean between El Salvador and Mexico. It is a mountainous country, the Sierra Madre stretching from east to west in its southern half. It is a land of huge forests in the north, many lakes and rivers and many volcanoes, at least one reaching an altitude of 12,000 feet. Guatemala City, established in 1776, is the third capital of Guatemala. The first capital was Ciudad Vieja which was almost destroyed by floods and an earthquake in 1542. The seat of government was moved to La Antigua; an earthquake in 1773 took its toll on this second capital city also, forcing the move to the present capital.

The official language is Spanish, but there are some 28 Mayan sects, so a number of Mayan-descended languages are also spoken. The population is almost thirteen million, mostly mestizos, usually referred to in Guatemala as ladinos, mixtures of Spanish and Mayan.

From about 500 BC the land we know as Guatemala, from a Nahuatl word meaning land of many trees, was the heart of the Mayan civilization, one of the most advanced civilizations of the ancient world. The Mayans created outstanding architectural works, temples, libraries, and pyramids, and there is evidence of literature and art, as well as mathematics and astronomy achievements. They and their primitive arms were no match, however, for the Spanish invaders, led by Pedro de Alvarado, who arrived with gunpowder and horses and in 1523-24 quickly overpowered the natives. The *conquistadores* burned the libraries and the Mayan cities, banned their religious observances, and forced the people into slave labor. Despite these great difficulties, the Mayans secretly retained their culture, their language, and their religion. Even today they wear hand-woven clothing decorated with symbols of their ancient heritage; they speak their own language—with more than twenty dialects—and they maintain their old religious celebrations.

Guatemala remained a colony of Spain for nearly three centuries. In 1821, along with other colonies in the area, Guatemala declared independence from Spain. For a short time it became the center of United Provinces of Central America, and in 1838 it became an independent republic.

Through the years Guatemala has suffered poverty and distress caused by unrest in government, many dictatorships, repression, rebellions, and civil wars, human rights violations, coups, and military rule, as well as earthquakes and other acts of nature.

✳ Christmas Traditions

Guatemaltecos, tecos as they call themselves, like other Latin Americans, begin decorating their homes and streets early in December. They build *pesebres*, often called *belenes*, some of them very elaborate with figures of people, animals, villages, and features of the countryside under and around their Christmas trees. And they prepare for *la quema del diablo*, an ancient tradition that is the real beginning of their Christmas season.

This burning of the devil occurs each year on December 7—at exactly six o'clock in the evening. In the week leading up to this important date, masked devils have appeared in the streets to chase and frighten the children. Houses have been cleaned from top to bottom. Items of no further use are collected and placed in front of each home where they are heaped into a pile and burned, the fire fed by *chiribiscos*, dry wood pieces gathered by the young children. This is to burn away symbolically all the evils of the past year and to welcome in a time of love and peace for the coming year. Besides the bonfires in front of every house, there is often a large fire in the village plaza where the devil is burned in effigy. All of this of course is accompanied by fireworks and music and dancing in the streets.

Las posadas chapinas on December 16 opens the traditional nine-day *posadas* in some parts of Guatemala. When they hear the sound of the drum, the *pitos* (whistles), the turtle shell rattles, and the marimbas, people rush into the streets to watch the procession. First comes a line of children carrying lanterns veiled in colored cellophane; next come those portraying Mary and Joseph seeking lodging in the village, as well as persons carrying religious statues. At the end of the parade often there is a statue representing God. Finally come many other men and women, young and old, praying and singing *villancicos*, accompanied always by marimba and *chirimía*, a double reed instrument similar to the oboe.

Las posadas continues for nine days. Each night the procession appears at the door of a different chosen house, where Joseph begs for shelter for the night. The landlord at first refuses, but finally, after a series of religious questions have been asked and satisfactorily answered, he permits them to enter. Tamales and punch are served, more singing and dancing lasting through many hours of the night. The figures of Mary and Joseph are left in the host house until the next night when the procedure resumes. Each night a different house is chosen until the last night when the most elaborate party is held.

When *la Nochebuena* arrives, friends and family gather to pray and to reflect on the holiday. They go to church in the evening, then come back for a feast of *tamales*. At midnight *el abrazo de Navidad* (the Christmas embrace) is exchanged, the children open their presents, and great quantities of fireworks are exploded.

Honduras

The Land and Its People

One of the largest countries in Central America, the Republic of Honduras lies between Nicaragua on the south and El Salvador and Guatemala on the west. The Caribbean Sea forms its northern border, and it has a very small access in the southwest to the Pacific Ocean. There are narrow coastal plains, but the interior of Honduras is mostly forested mountains. The capital city is Tegucigalpa. The population is about seven million. Spanish is the official and predominant language; ninety per cent of its seven million citizens are mestizos, of mixed European and native Indian heritage.

When the Spanish conquered the natives of Honduras, as well as those of other Central American lands, they needed strategies to bring peaceful cooperation among the various ethnic groups in order to accomplish their goals of mining precious metals and converting the people to Christianity. One of their earliest and most successful plans was the establishment of the *guancasco*, a ceremony of peace between warring villages, a rite of music and dance still celebrated in some areas two or three times a year, now as a feast of friendship.

Every village has its own patron saint, and the custom of celebrating the feast day of that saint has continued for hundreds of years, sometimes for a day, sometimes for as long as a week. A saint revered by all *catrachos*, the Honduran people, is *la Virgen de Suyapa*, the patron of Honduras. Processions with fireworks, music, and dancing feature prominently in the fiestas in honor of her, as well as those for all patronal saints.

The western valleys of Honduras were the homeland of Mayan peoples from at least 1,000 BC. Evidence suggests that around 500-800 AD there were as many as fifteen thousand people living here. Like that of other Mayan groups, the area was mysteriously abandoned about 900 AD, but there are still many remains of Mayan sculpture and architecture in the area.

Columbus first came to Honduras in 1502 on his fourth and last voyage. Although Juan Diaz de Solís and Vicente Yañez may have stopped there briefly in 1508, it was not until 1524 that Spanish conquest of the land we know as Honduras really began. In that year, just a few years after his conquest of the great valley of Mexico, Hernán Cortez sent Cristóbal de Olid to lay claim to the land. Natives, especially the Lencas, fiercely resisted Spanish colonization, but they were ultimately overcome and a Spanish stronghold developed.

The deep Honduras Bay and nearby islands off the northern shore created a haven for British and Dutch pirates in the seventeenth century. After gold and silver were discovered in the interior and loaded onto Spanish ships for return to Europe, pirate ships were frequently waiting to attack. Pirates were also among those responsible for bringing hundreds of Africans to Honduras, where they were forced into slave labor in order to harvest great quantities of mahogany for European use.

Honduras achieved independence from Spain, with other American colonies, in 1821 and at first was a part of Mexico. It later became a member of the Central American Federation, but in 1838 it became an independent republic. Like citizens of other middle American countries, Hondurans have suffered through poverty, devastating acts of nature, and political unrest, but in spite of all it is said that Honduras is recognized as among the most peaceful, forward-looking countries in Central America and its people among the friendliest in the world.

✲✲ Christmas Traditions

Like other Latin Americans, Hondurans build elaborate *nacimientos* in their homes, often an entire village in the living room, sometimes taking up the entire room. The Nativity scene with the Holy Family, *los misterios,* is in the center, but all around are scenes resembling the villages the builders themselves live in, with figures of people, animals, buildings made of clay, wood, or paper. Favorite toys of the children are included—Superman, Batman, Wonder Woman. The miniature village often reflects something from the occurrences of the past year. For instance, after Hurricane Mitch struck with destructive force in 1998, most of the *nacimientos* had a section reminding them of the hurricane that had destroyed many houses.

Christmas trees are made of small branches wrapped in cotton and decorated. In the past few years artificial Christmas trees as we know them have become popular. And—of course—fireworks!

The nine days of *las posadas,* Joseph and Mary's search for lodging, are observed when groups of singers go each night to a designated house to ask for shelter.

On Christmas Day at dawn the figure of *el Niño* is removed, "kidnapped," from someone's house, and the observance of *la desaparición del Niño Jesús,* the disappearance of the Baby Jesus, begins. Between December 26 and 30 all the friends and neighbors set out to find the image. When it is discovered in someone else's house, that homeowner is obliged to create a big fiesta for all who helped in the search.

Garifunas, the Black Caribs of Honduras's north coast, begin the Christmas dance season on the afternoon of December 24 with the arrival of the Christmas herald, Warini. His body covered with plants and accompanied by singers and two drummers, this solo male dancer makes appearances all over town, announcing the season. He will dance once more on Jnauary 6. Women's dance groups sing and dance all night on Christmas Eve and New Year's Eve while the men are their accompanying drummers. Their principal song/dance form is solo and response, accompanied by drums, maracas, and conch shell horns, reminiscent of their African heritage.

Young Garifuna girls, in groups of 30 to 60 perform *pastorelas,* shepherds' plays, in which they go from house to house singing to the Baby in each home's crèche, from Christmas Eve until January 6. Their accompaniment is the click of their shepherds' staves.

Christmas Day among the Garifunas brings—instead of Santa—*el indio bárbaro* (bearded Indian) and the *máscaro* (masked) dancers. *El indio bárbaro* is covered in red anetto seeds, oil, and clay. He carries a bow and arrow with which he threatens to paint bystanders with the anetto seed mixture if they refuse to give him money. He does not speak but uses a whistle to capture attention. His whistle and the screams of children are heard all day as he chases the children through the streets.

Dressed sometimes in women's clothing, usually in black and white, the *máscaro* dancers are masked men who dance the *wanaragua*, the Dance of Warriors, known in other places as *joncanu*, John Canoe. This energetic dance begins with a circle of dancers; in turn each comes to the center for a short improvised solo movement.

A unique Garifuna custom not observed exclusively at Christmas is the *palo volador*, pole flyer, in which one or two men climb a tall pole, about forty feet high, wind rope around their bodies, tie the rope to the top of the pole, and then jump, unwinding themselves as they descend to the ground.

Nicaragua

The Land and Its People

The Republic of Nicaragua, about the size of New York, is the largest country in Central America. It is sandwiched between Honduras and Costa Rica, with shorelines on both the Pacific Ocean and the Gulf of Mexico. Its capital city is Managua, and its population is almost six million. The land can be divided into three distinct geographic areas: Pacific lowlands, north central mountains, and the Miskito coast. While the western part of the nation is populated largely by people of Spanish descent, the eastern side is made up of creoles and mestizos, mixtures of Miskito Indians and Blacks who were brought to the area as slaves, and some native Garifunas, the Black Caribs from Honduras.

Nicaragua is a land beset with active volcanoes—at least forty—as well as hurricanes and earthquakes. An outstanding feature of the country is Lago de Nicaragua which has a great variety of aquatic life. The official language is Spanish, but English and various native dialects are widely spoken.

First seen by Europeans in 1502 when Columbus's expedition sailed past its eastern coast, Nicaragua had been the home of Aztec/Mayan-related natives for hundreds of years. In 1522 Spanish explorer Gil González Dávila, coming south from Mexico, was at first welcomed by the village chiefs who gave him gifts of gold and led the natives in converting to Christianity. As González advanced into the interior however, he met hostile chiefs and quickly retreated to Mexico, bearing his gifts of gold and pearls. Two years later, in 1524, the first permanent settlements were established, and the country was named for the chief of the area's leading tribe, Nicarao.

The United States has played a part in Nicaragua's history at least since 1912 when it sent Marines to "support the government." During this time the United States was considering the possibility of a canal through Nicaragua that would link the Gulf of Mexico and the Pacific Ocean. Violence and disorder erupted in 1924, and American marines returned in 1927, staying until 1933 when the Somoza regime seemed to be firmly established.

Somoza and his sons who succeeded him, ruled under a dictatorship until 1979 when the liberal, pro-communist Sandinistas seized power, ousted the Somoza regime, and began wide-ranging education and health reforms. The country was the scene of revolution and civil war between the Sandinistas and the Contras, who were funded secretly by the United States, throughout the 1980s.

The war was over and the political scene became calmer in the 1990s. Unfortunately the tragedy of Hurricane Mitch in 1998, in which more than 10,000 people were killed and millions of dollars in damage was suffered, interrupted the economic rebuilding of the country.

✳ Christmas Traditions

Nicaragua's Christmas season really begins in late November with preparations for the great feast of *la purísima*. Elaborate altars are made in honor of the Virgin Mary, crèches are prepared in private homes, and front doors are left open so that passersby can see inside and enter to sing and pray with the home owners. The eve of *la purísima*, December 7, is the time for *la gritería*, the calling, a time for enthusiastic yelling and general uproar, then for loud, joyful singing. There is a great display of fireworks and music as the streets fill with people of all ages, singing *villancicos* and *aguinaldos* outside each house where an altar is visible. Children bring bouquets of flowers, especially poinsettias, *flores de pastor* or *flores de nochebuena*, and sing songs to *la Virgen*. The special *purísima* gifts they receive in return are sweets made from sugar cane, *pinolillo* and *chicha de maíz*, Nicaraguan beverages.

A novena begins on December 16 and ends on *Nochebuena*, corresponding to the time for *las posadas*. The pilgrims seek shelter at a selected house each night. When finally they are invited in, there is a great party with food and drink for everyone and a piñata for the children to break.

In most homes Christmas Eve is spent preparing the great feast, *la cena de Nochebuena*. Especially in rural areas there are many colorful processions with representations of Biblical characters—kings, Romans, apostles, and many others. These processions also include *la gigantona*, the giant woman, an enormous puppet on stilts, about twelve feet tall, representing a queen and serving as a reverential symbol of the Virgin Mary. *La gigantona* is accompanied by a dancing partner, *el enano*, the dwarf, who is of normal height.

Another tradition is *el aguinaldo*, a Christmas bonus given to all workers by their employers, an important gift of money.

La cena for family and friends occurs either in the evening of the 24th or after mass. Church bells ring out the call to midnight mass, *la misa de aguinaldo* or *la misa de gallo*. At the end of the mass many stand in line to kiss the image of the Christ Child, then all return home to add the Baby to the crèche, to open a few presents that *el Niño Dios* has brought, and to wish everybody *unas felices pascuas* or *feliz Navidad*. There are more fireworks, more singing and dancing—sometimes until dawn.

On New Year's Eve much of this is repeated. There are fireworks and street performers and festive meals with friends and family. An interesting custom that some observe at midnight is a fortune-telling device. An egg is broken into a glass of water, mixed, and looked at carefully to discover an image that will give a clue to what the new year holds.

On Jaunary 5, the eve of the Epiphany, *el día de Tres Reyes*, again there are fireworks and parades. A special cake, *rosca de Reyes*, Kings' cake, is shaped like a crown with candied fruit embedded as jewels. A small doll representing the Christ Child hiding from King Herod on the day of Holy Innocents is baked into the cake. The person finding the doll must be host to a party for everyone on February 2, the day of Candlemas. At bedtime on this night children fill their shoes with straw and place them where the Three Kings will be sure to see them and to trade gifts for the straw the children have left for the camels.

Panamá

The Land and Its People

Panamá is a small country, about the size of South Carolina, the most southern country of Central America, important as a bridge between continents as well as between oceans. Its eastern border is Costa Rica, its western border the South American country of Colombia. The Gulf of Mexico is on its northern side and the Pacific Ocean on its southern side. It is a land filled with rugged mountains, rain forests, jungles, white sand beaches. Its highest point, 11,400 feet, is the dormant Volcán de Chiriqui. Thanks to rain from May to December, flowers and birds flourish. The rain forests provide a home for more than 1200 varieties of orchids and 933 species of birds.

There are about three million Panamanian citizens. The capital is Panamá City, established first in 1519, sacked by the British pirate Henry Morgan in the mid-1600s and rebuilt in 1673. Spanish is the official language, but English is widely spoken, as are several native tongues. Panamá's people are largely mestizo, but there are also significant percentages of native Indian groups.

Present-day Panamá was not discovered by the Spaniards until Columbus's fourth visit in 1502. Its ideal position for Spain's aims in the New World was soon apparent, and by 1510, with the establishment of Nombre de Dios on the Caribbean coast, it was beginning to serve as a headquarters for exploring north into the riches of the Aztecs and south into the even greater riches of the Incas. From here the invaders were able to spread their conquest through Central America and Mexico as well as into the lands we now know as Colombia, Perú, Chile, and other parts of South America. When the Inca empire collapsed, their vast stores of gold were quickly taken by their conquerors up the Pacific coast to Panamá then carried overland to Nombre de Dios where they were loaded onto ships bound for Spain.

Nombre de Dios came to be the home port for Spain's *Terra Firma* treasure fleet, established early in the sixteenth century as a trading plan in which ships loaded with manufactured goods from Europe would sail twice a year to the colonies in the Caribbean, sell their goods, then be filled with the gold and silver mined in the new land to be taken to the Crown in Spain. By the mid to late years of that century pirates lurked in the area, waiting to attack the mineral-laden ships en route to Spain, and the entire system eventually collapsed.

Panamá, along with other Spanish colonies, became independent from Spain in 1821. Instead of becoming an independent nation at that time, however, it became a province of Colombia. It was not until 1903, with the serious interest of the United States in building a canal from the Caribbean to the Pacific, that the Colombian province seceded and became the Republic of Panamá.

The building of the canal is an interesting story. As early as 1524 it was suggested to Spanish King Carlos V that a canal should be dug on this narrow isthmus, and a plan was drawn up for it, but other matters intervened. Three hundred years later Spain again became interested but did nothing to effect a plan. In 1848 another event occurred which piqued the interest of many nations: the discovery of gold in California. Finally in 1903, supported by the United States, Panamá seceded from Colombia and immediately signed a treaty with the United States to permit a perpetual lease on a ten-mile strip of land that would link the two bodies of water. In return the United States would guarantee protection of the new republic, make an initial payment of ten million dollars and promise an annual payment of $250,000. By 1914 the canal was completed. The Canal Zone was operated by the United States until 1999 when it was turned over to the Panamanian people.

⁂ Christmas Traditions

El día de las madres on December 8 begins the Panamanian celebration of Christmastide. By that date Christmas trees decorated with lights and ribbons and colorful ornaments have been put up in most homes. In many areas of the country there are contests to choose the most attractive decorations. Houses are thoroughly cleaned, often repainted, and preparations are begun for the festive *cena* for family and friends on Christmas Eve.

On December 21 *el espíritu de la Navidad* is observed as a time of reflection in which believers remember their sins and ask for pardon. They make every effort to remember any wrong they have done to any person and then to apologize and do some act of penance to make their apology meaningful. After this exercise of creating *el corazón limpio* (the clean heart), it is time to pray for favors of health for friends and family, for country, for peace in the world, and for whatever else is hoped for. These desires are written on special papers and saved. When one of the prayers is answered, its paper is burned and there is a prayer of thanksgiving.

Christmas Eve mass begins in some parts of the country at 10 p.m., but in most places it is the *misa de gallo* beginning at midnight. After mass and after the *abrazos de Navidad*, the *cena* begins—turkey or ham, *tamales*, potato salad, special *postres* (desserts), non-alcoholic *piñas coladas*. Parents scurry around to place the children's gifts under the Christmas tree so the children can open them after the meal. Later the older young people go out to dance through the night.

In many parts of Panamá a folk tradition called *los bundes* is observed during the Christmas season. Beginning on December 8 participants go from house to house, carrying a colorfully decorated urn topped with an image of *el Niño Dios* in which to collect donations that will be used in the final celebration on Christmas Eve. One home and its family have been chosen for the honor of housing and caring for *el Niño* during the coming year, and on Christmas Eve it is delivered to the chosen home and given a place of honor. Townspeople then crowd the streets and, accompanied by fireworks and candles, walk in procession to the privileged home. Here the woman of the house holds the image in her arms as all the women who have come in the procession pass, two by two, in front of it, singing *villancicos*. Then the party begins with good food and drink and much singing and dancing. But this is not the end of *los bundes*, for the special dance called by that name begins, not to end except for urgent working hours until *el día de Reyes* on January 6. There will be dancing beginning in the afternoons and continuing through entire nights until almost dawn. Accompaniment to the dancing comes from a large box struck with two mallets at the same time, a hand drum, and a pair of maracas.

On the 27th children go with red crosses painted on their faces and carrying long wooden staffs to beg money and candy from their neighbors. On the next day brightly-costumed, masked revelers take to the streets to play harmless pranks on their friends, especially trying to frighten the children with rubber snakes and rats, shooting people with water guns and shaving cream cans.

Mexico

The center of the newfound world, Nueva España, as well as the center of the American continents, is the land we know today as Mexico. The reasons for conquest were many and varied. Attributed to Spain, but no doubt oversimplified, were "God, gold, and glory" as motives for the conquest of New Spain. Glory came—and went. Gold was present in abundance in some places, completely lacking in others. But the quest for saving souls, for converting the natives to Christianity never faltered, and it caused the land of conquest to extend farther and farther from its point of first encounter.

It was from this center that Spanish conquest and colonization spread, first to the south, then to the north, to comprise a vast land that covered most of the known western hemisphere years before other Europeans joined them. For about three hundred years allegiance was pledged to Spain, though the connection between old and new worlds became more and more tenuous as the years passed. After the break from Spain, the boundaries of the land that was Mexico soon were reconfigured as the young upstart nation, the United States of America, entered the picture and claimed great sections of the land.

The Land and Its People

Los estados unidos mexicanos—the United Mexican States—about one-fifth the size of its northern neighbor, the other United States, has a population of nearly 109,000,000, at least nineteen million of whom live in its capital, Mexico City. Mexico is bordered on the west by the Pacific Ocean, on the east by the Gulf of Mexico and the Caribbean Sea, with neighboring countries Guatemala and Belize on the south and east, and the United States on the north.

Mexico is the fourteenth largest country in the world, the eleventh most populous, and the world's most populous Spanish-speaking country. It comprises thirty-one states and the federal district Mexico City.

The land varies from high desert in the north to tropical lowlands in the south. Two extensions of the Rocky Mountains traverse its length, the Sierra Madre Oriental and the Sierra Madre Occidental. The Cordillera Neovolcánica bisects the country east to west. Its high plateaus and mountain chains and its ocean front lowlands make it a land of great biodiversity. Two outstanding features especially attractive as tourist destinations are the peninsula of Baja California on the west and the Yucatán Peninsula on the east.

Mexico is the ancestral home of the Olmec, Maya, Toltec, and Aztec peoples, and it is the place in the New World where most of the European colonizing and populating began, the viceroyalty of New Spain.

Scholars generally believe the first humans in America were Asians who walked across a land bridge over the Bering Strait thousands of years ago. There is evidence of hunter/gatherer cultures in Mexico from around 11,000 BC and suggestions that corn, beans, and squash were cultivated many millennia ago. By 1500 BC clay figures and pottery were being produced.

First of the great civilizations, the Maya, having cultural ties to the earlier Olmecs, flourished between 200 and 900 AD, the Classic

Period, the Mayan Golden Age. They developed a discipline of writing, a sophisticated system of mathematics that recorded time, and without the use of metal tools they created architectural wonders, many remains of which can be seen even today.

The most important sites of the Classic Period are Teotihuacán in Mexico City, Monte Albán in Oaxaca, and Mayan complexes in Chiapas, Tabasco, Campeche, and Yucatán. When Teotihuacán was destroyed by unknown events and for unknown reasons in 650, the Yucatán Peninsula became the new center for the Mayans until about 900, after which rapid decline of the civilization set in.

The Post Classic period saw a surge of militarism, with fortifications and wars rampant. Three groups, the Toltec in central Mexico and the Zapotec and Mixtec in southern Mexico, rose and fell until the last arrivals entered the Valley of Mexico in the early 1300s. The Aztecs, according to their creation story, came from Aztlán, guided by the hummingbird sounds of their god Ituitzilopichtitl to the marshy islands of Lake Texcoco, present day Mexico City, where they saw an eagle perched on a cactus, holding a snake in its mouth. This, according to their ancient lore, was a sign to settle in this place. So they built Tenochitlán on one of the islands. A monarchy with King Acamapichtli was established by 1376, and by the early sixteenth century the Aztecs dominated the area. Their successful social structure was built on a four-part complex: the nobility and high priests, including military and political leaders; the merchant class who carried on all business and who lived apart from the others; commoners who were civil servants; and farmers and slaves.

Who knows to what heights the Aztecs might have risen but for the events of 1519 that set the course of their destiny?

Accompanied by seven hundred men with guns and horses and with interpreters who could speak and translate Mayan, Nahuatl, and Spanish, having heard of great wealth in the interior, Hernán Cortés sailed from Cuba in 1519. It was as if the empereor Moctezuma expected him because among the Aztecs there was a long-held belief that the god Quetzlcóatl, the plumed serpent, would return to the people in the form of a white god coming from the east. To his peril Moctezuma welcomed Cortés into Tenochitlán, feeling that the invading Spaniards fulfilled the prophecy.

The welcome was soon regretted, for in a short time Cortés arrested Moctezuma, imprisoned him, and eventually executed him.

Skirmishes between natives and invaders continued, but by 1521 Cortés had conquered the city, captured the last Aztec emperor, Cuauhtémoc, and all of the Aztec empire. The greater force of Spanish arms as well as the introduction of diseases to which the Indians had no immunity and which caused the death of many, took their toll and brought about complete defeat. Cuauhtémoc became a symbol of honor and courage, the first Mexican national hero.

Here in the geographic center of the New World the viceroyalty of New Spain was established, and from here scores of expeditions were sent out over the next three hundred years to explore the vast unknown lands to the north. Cortés built his colony on top of the ruins of Tenochitlán and called it Mexico.

Throughout the seventeenth and eighteenth centuries more and more Spaniards came to Mexico. *Encomiendas*—in which grants of land and native slaves were given to citizens in repayment for their loyalty to the government—had been successfully established earlier in Santo Domingo and Cuba, and now they were to prove their value in Mexico. The system served both ways: *encomenderos* were required to take care of their slaves and to help them assimilate into Spanish culture and Roman Catholicism, in return for which the slaves worked for their masters. Disease and hardship continued to wipe out great numbers of natives, and African slaves were brought in to replace the Indians.

Trouble developed between *gauchapines* or *peninsulares*, those born in Spain, and *criollos*, those of Spanish ancestry born in the New World. Social classes inevitably began to develop and with them the seeds of rebellion and revolution which would play prominently in the next two centuries.

As explorations expanded, Spain laid claim to vast areas of land north of the seat of government in the viceroyalty of New Spain. But, as in all parts of Spain's discoveries in the western hemisphere, the people of Mexico, especially natives and *criollos*, were growing restless, and on September 16, 1810, *el diez y seis de septiembre*, they declared independence from Spain and began the Mexican Revolution which lasted until independence was finally won in 1821 and the republic was proclaimed in 1822.

The next years were turbulent times. Mexico now controlled all the land we know today as Texas, California, Nevada, Utah, Arizona, New Mexico, and parts of Colorado and Wyoming, as well as Mexico proper. Meanwhile the United States was expanding south and west, and when they were granted settlement rights, colonists from the United States began pouring into Texas.

By 1835 *americanos* outnumbered *mexicanos* four to one, and there was a strong push for Texas to secede from Mexico. After the Mexican army under General Santa Anna defeated the Texans in bloody battles at the Alamo and Goliad, American forces led by Sam Houston, responded by ambushing the Mexicans near the San Jacinto River, defeating them soundly, and capturing Santa Anna. While he was under custody, Santa Anna signed two treaties, one promising to withdraw all Mexican forces to positions south of the Rio Grande, the other recognizing the independence of Texas. Texas was annexed by the United States in 1845, exacerbating troubled relations between the United States and Mexico.

It was probably inevitable that these two young nations—the United States about fifty years old and Mexico even younger, each with internal unrest of its own—would continue to have territorial disagreements. Now various diplomatic problems arose. The Mexican congress had never ratified the treaties Santa Anna signed and it annulled them by passing a law, to be observed retroactively, that no treaty signed by a Mexican negotiator while in captivity would be honored. In addition, Texas claimed a large area of land that had been a part of Mexico, and New Spain, since the days of the *conquistadores*.

War broke out in April 1846. The United States Army under

General Stephen W. Kearney occupied California and New Mexico. General Zachary Taylor led forces into northern Mexico where there was fierce fighting with Santa Anna's armies. The third front, the Army of Occupation led by General Winfield Scott, was an invasion of Vera Cruz, leading to a brief occupation of Mexico City. The war continued until Mexico's surrender in the final Battle of Chapultepec in September 1847.

Peace negotiations culminated in the Treaty of Guadalupe Hidalgo, February 2, 1848, and the final boundaries of Mexico were set. According to this agreement the Rio Grande was the established boundary between the two countries, Mexico surrendered all her land north of the Rio Grande for which the United States agreed to pay fifteen million dollars in compensation and settle claims of private citizens against Mexico.

But Mexico's troubles with foreign powers were not over. After the war, its treasury depleted, the Mexican government under President Benito Juárez declared a moratorium on all foreign debt repayments in 1861. France, Britain, and Spain responded by sending troops to Vera Cruz to enforce debt collection. When they were unable to find agreement among themselves, Britain and Spain withdrew, and France occupied the country, seizing the opportunity to establish an empire in the New World.

Fierce warfare ensued. An important victory for the Mexicans occurred at Puebla on May 5, 1862, when General Ignacio Zaragoza routed the French forces. To this day both *cinco de mayo* and *el diez y seis de septiembre* are observed as Mexico's two national holidays. But this victory was not enough to end the war. The French continued their march to Mexico City and their occupation of Mexico.

In 1864 Ferdinand Maximilian Joseph von Hapsburg of Austria became emperor of Mexico. Emperor Maximilian I and the Empress Carlotta soon found themselves beset on every hand by enemies, and from the beginning it appeared the empire was doomed. In 1867 Maximilian surrendered to rebel forces, was tried under Juárez's orders and executed.

The next years saw remarkable economic growth under the leadership of Porfirio Díaz but also political repression and economic inequality, sparking the Mexican Revolution of 1910. After this war, in the remainder of the first half of the twentieth century, a period called *el milagro mexicano* (the Mexican miracle) there occurred more gains in the economy even though there was continued social and economic inequality with extremes of wealth and poverty.

NAFTA, the North Atlantic Free Trade Agreement, a trade bloc whose members are Mexico, the United States, and Canada, was established in 1994. This agreement has canceled most tariffs between and among the countries, and protection for workers and the environment has been a consideration. Though not without its critics, NAFTA has shown very positive results in trade and industry, especially in Mexico, though its effects on agriculture are more problematic.

✳ Christmas Traditions

The kings of Spain saw to it that priests and brothers—Franciscans, Jesuits, Augustinians, Benedictines, Dominicans—were supplied with all their needs and that they accompanied every group of explorers or colonists, for their supreme and unique mission was to convert the natives to Christianity. They went about their work zealously, using any and all available means to convert the native populations they encountered.

One highly effective way to interest the Indians in the new religion was to show parallels of Christian events and personae to those of the Aztec pantheon. Three of these parallels, devotion to *la Virgen de Guadalupe*, *las posadas*, and the *piñata*, began in the Old World, spread throughout the New World, finally came to be especially associated with Mexico, and are very important Christmas traditions.

La Virgen de Guadalupe

The birth of Huitzilopochtli, principal god of the Aztecs, was celebrated in *panquetzaliztli* (December), according to the Aztec calendar. This made a convenient parallel in time to celebrate with the natives the birth also of the Christian God. On a hill near Tenochtitlan called Tepeyac there was a temple honoring Tonantzin, the mother goddess. This too would prove significant in the missionaries' work with the natives.

Throughout the centuries of Christianity devout souls have reported visitations from the Virgin Mary. Of particular interest are one in Spain in 1325 and one in Mexico two hundred years later, in 1537.

It is true the celebration honoring the Virgin of Guadalupe is not actually a Christmas tradition, but the time it occurs, December 12, is significant, and many Latin Americans begin their *navidades* with the Feast of the Immaculate Conception on December 8. Their holiday celebrations then continue with no letup through *Nochebuena* and Christmas Day and on through Twelfth Night.

According to legend, in the first century Saint Luke carved a black wooden image of the Virgin holding a baby. The statue was buried with him in Asia Minor. Sometime in the fourth century his relics, and the statue, were moved to Constantinople. The image became known as a marvelous healing icon. From here it traveled to Rome and made its way into the hands of Pope Gregory the Great (590-604) who presented it as a gift to Saint Leander, Bishop of Seville. Miracles continued to be credited to the Dark Madonna as she came to be known.

When the Muslims invaded Seville in 711, she was spirited away by men of the church and hidden somewhere in the hills of Extremadura. As centuries passed, the little statue was forgotten until the year 1325.

When a humble shepherd, Gil Cordero, discovered one of the cows from his flock was missing, he went searching along the Guadalupe River where he found it, apparently dead. As he made preparations to remove the hide to take to his employer, the animal suddenly jumped up, alive and well. At that moment there appeared before Gil the Virgin Mary who ordered him to tell the priests that in this place they would find the image that had been buried so long ago.

The image was recovered and a small shelter was built over it. Miracles once again began to occur, paralyzed limbs regained movement, pain was relieved, illnesses disappeared. Her fame spread and health-seekers began making pilgrimages to pray before the small image. A more fitting home was built for her, and by the middle of the fifteenth century the Basilica of Guadalupe had been completed and had become one of Spain's most important pilgrimage sites.

It was here at *el Monasterio de Santa María de Guadalupe* that Queen Isabella and King Ferdinand gave Columbus authority to make his first voyage in 1492, and it was to this place that he brought back natives converted to Christianity to be baptized in the basilica dedicated to the Virgin of Guadalupe who became patroness of the New World and of all *hispanidad*.

Now fast forward two hundred years to Saturday, December 9, 1531, an Indian convert, Cuautlatóhuac, known after his conversion as Juan Diego, was hurrying down Tepeyac Hill on his way to mass to pray for his uncle, Juan Bernardino, who was gravely ill. Suddenly there appeared before him a beautiful woman who identified herself as the Mother of God and told Juan Diego to ask Bishop Zumárraga to build a temple where she stood at the foot of Tepeyac.

Juan Diego hurried to the bishop with her request. His story was met with disbelief and skepticism. Could the lady send a sign, the bishop asked, to verify her story?

Juan Diego saw her again that evening and on Sunday. He spent Monday caring for his uncle. On Tuesday, December 12, at daybreak he was hurrying to find a priest to give his uncle last rites when the Virgin Mary again appeared before him. She reassured him that she had also visited his uncle and that he would be well.

Juan Diego told her of the bishop's skepticism and his request for a sign that *la Virgen* had actually appeared and spoken to Juan Diego. She then told him to gather roses among the nearby rocks. He knew December was not the time, nor the rocks of Tepeyac the place, to find roses, but he went looking—and he found them. He gathered the roses in his *tilma* (cape) and returned to the Holy Mother. She rearranged them, wrapped them carefully in the *tilma*, and sent him back to the bishop.

When Juan Diego met the bishop, he opened his *tilma* and beautiful, fresh, dew-sprinkled Castilian roses fell from it. The bishop and his attendants fell to their knees as they looked at the roses and the lifesize image of the Virgin Mary that appeared on the *tilma*.

Juan Diego did not see Our Lady again, but a shrine was built at Tepeyac Hill, and people immediately began coming to worship. Since that time nearly five hundred years ago a grand basilica has been erected. The *tilma* remains the focus of attention for hundreds of thousands of worshipers.

Why is she called Guadalupe? It is said she identified herself to Juan Bernardino as the Virgin of Coatlaxopeuh, pronounced *quat-la-su-peh,* sounding somewhat like *Guadalupe.* It is reasonable to assume that not only Columbus but other explorers of the time knew and revered the earlier Virgin of Guadalupe and that they, especially the Franciscans who accompanied them, spread the word wherever they went. It is also reasonable to assume that *Coatlaxopeuh* slipped easily into *Guadalupe,* a word that had become familiar to the Indians and certainly was remembered and honored by the Spanish.

In "Christmas Holidays in Mexico: Festivals of Light, Love, and Peace," Judy King writes: "The devotion to Guadalupe transcends any form of religious scope to become a symbol of Mexican nationalism and patriotism. Guadalupe creates a bond, a sense of being Mexican, of profound pride in being Mexican. Her influence crosses all borders and boundaries."

Las Posadas

Another Christmas tradition shared by many but having its American genesis in colonial Mexico is *las posadas*, the dramatization of *los santos peregrinos* (the Holy Pilgrims) making their way from Nazareth to Bethlehem, seeking shelter and a place for the impending birth of Jesus.

It is said that Saint Ignacio Loyola in sixteenth century Spain was the first to suggest a Christmas novena, nine days of special prayers, the nine days corresponding to Mary's nine months of pregnancy before Jesus was born. In 1580 Saint John of the Cross developed the idea of a religious dramatization of the event.

In 1586 Friar Diego de Soria from Acolman, a Mexican Augustinian Monastery, was able to obtain a papal bull from Pope Sixtus V ordering that a *misa de aguinaldo* (Christmas gift mass), novenas on the nine days preceding Christmas Day, December 16-24, be instituted in Mexico. At first these were held in the church, and only gradually did *las posadas* evolve into the present form associated more with individual houses than with the church building.

This was still another way to show honor to the Aztec god Huiotzilopchtil in *panquetzaliztli*, the month both his birth and the winter solstice were observed, while at the same time celebrating the birth of the Christian God.

The songs associated with the observance of *las posadas* are sung by two choruses, *los peregrinos* outside the inn and *los hosteleros* (the innkeepers) inside.

While there are many variants in the specifics, the principal ingredients of *las posadas* remain the same: Saint Joseph leading the Virgin Mary on a burro, followed by shepherds, angels, animals, a star either at the beginning or the end of the procession. Sometimes children are the actors; sometimes small statues of the main characters are carried.

Usually three or four homes have been designated as places where the procession will stop to ask for *posada*. Singing as they move along, the group knocks at the door of the first house and sings the request for shelter. The *hostelero* sings his refusal. The group moves on to the next house, and the process is repeated. This may happen once again at a third house, or it may have been decided that the third stop will be the place where the pilgrims are granted entry. As the song changes to "*Entren santos peregrinos,*" the host welcomes the group into his home. More carols are sung, the rosary recited, and other prayers offered. At last the *piñata* is broken, and punch, tamales, and sweets are served. The activities are repeated on eight more nights, and the grandest part of all happens on *Nochebuena*.

Following are the two songs most commonly associated with the observance of *las posadas*.

Las Posadas

Mexico

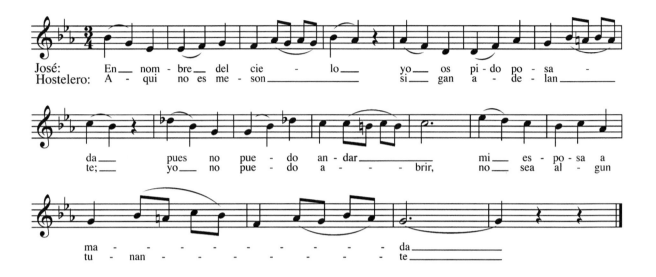

José: En nom - bre del cie - lo yo os pi - do po - sa -
Hostelero: A - qui no es me - son si - gan a - de - lan

da pues no pue - do an - dar mi es - po - sa a
te; yo no pue - do a - brir, no sea al - gun

ma - da
tu - nan - te

1. José: In the name of heaven I beg you for lodging, for she cannot walk, my beloved wife.
   Hostelero: This is not an inn, so keep going. I cannot open; you may be a rogue.

2. José: No seas inhumano, tennos caridad, que el Dios de los cielos te lo premiará.
   Don't be inhuman, have mercy on us; God of the heavens will reward you for it.
   Hostelero: Ya se pueden ir y no me molestar porque si me enfado os voy a apalear.
   You can go on now and don't bother us, because if I become annoyed, I'll give you a thrashing.

3. José: Venimos rendidos desde Nazaret, yo soy carpintero de nombre José.
   We are worn out coming from Nazareth. I am a carpenter, Joseph by name.
   Hostelero: No me importa el nombre, déjenme dormir, pues que yo les digo que no hemos de abrir.
   I don't care about your name; let me sleep, because I already told you we will not open up.

4. José: Posada te pide, amado casero, por solo una noche la Reina del Cielo.
   The Queen of Heaven is asking you, dear sir, for lodging for just one night.
   Hostelero: Pues si es una reina quien lo solicita, ¿cómo es que de noche anda tan solita?
   Well, if it's a queen who asks, why is it at night that she travels so alone?

5. José: Mi esposa es María, es Reina del Cielo y madre va a ser del Divino Verbo.
   My wife is Mary, the Queen of Heaven and she will be the mother of the Divine Word.
   Hostelero: ¿eres tú José? ¿tu esposa María? Entren, peregrinos, no los conocía.
   Are you Joseph? Your wife Mary? Enter, pilgrims; I did not recognize you.

6. José: Dios pague, señores, vuestra caridad, y que os colme el cielo de felicidad.
   May God reward your charity, gentle people, and thus heaven heap happiness on you.
   Hostelero: ¡Dichosa la casa que alberga este día a la Virgen pura, la Hermosa María!
   Blessed is the house that shelters this day the pure Virgin, the beautiful Mary.

Enter holy pilgrims; receive this little corner, not of this poor dweling, but from my heart.

In Oaxaca on *la Nochebuena, las posadas* ends with *calendas* (processions) that start from individual churches, forming a giant parade that circles the *zócalo* (plaza), then returns, each to the church from which it started. The *calendas* feature large banners painted with religious scenes— another teaching procedure started by the early priests—floats, paper lanterns carried on poles, smaller *farolitos* (little lanterns), giant puppet-like figures parading on stilts.

When the *calendas* return to their churches, *la acostada del Niño* (putting the Baby Jesus to bed) occurs as they place the figure in the prepared *nacimiento* just before midnight mass. After mass there are rockets and fireworks of all kinds, and then all go home for the Christmas dinner.

La Piñata

Even the *piñata*, which at first seems totally secular, was used to teach and convert the Indians, each part of it having religious significance.

Marco Polo is credited with bringing the *piñata* from China, its place of origin, to Italy in his thirteenth and fourteenth century travels to the Orient. The Chinese *piñata*, shaped in animal forms, decorated with colored paper, and filled with seeds was a part of the New Year's festivity. After the *piñata* was broken, the remains were burned and the ashes gathered for good luck in the coming year.

The first European home of the *piñata* was Italy where it became a part of Lenten observance. When it spread to Spain, the Dance of the *Piñata* was observed the first Sunday of Lent.

Spanish missionaries discovered very soon after their arrival in the early sixteenth century that a somewhat similar tradition existed among the natives as a part of the celebration for their god Huitzilopochtli's birthday celebration. A pot decorated with colorful feathers and filled with small treasures was placed high on a pole, to be broken by blindfolded stick-wielders.

This event occurring in late December transferred easily into the Spanish *piñata* and its religious significance. A clay pot, *olla*, also called *cántaro*, represented Satan. It was lavishly decorated with bright paper streamers, making "Satan" attractive to those who saw it. The traditional shape had seven points to represent the seven deadly sins, gluttony, greed, lust, sloth, pride, envy, and wrath. Inside the *olla* were placed candies and fruits to represent the temptations of the world.

The three theological virtues are represented. *Faith* is blind, just as the participant attempting to break the *piñata* is blindfolded. The *piñata* is hung above the heads of the watchers, so they look heavenward in *hope* for the prize. *Charity* is symbolized in everyone's sharing the gifts the *piñata* holds.

Through the centuries the *piñata* has lost much of its religious significance, but it retains its popularity as a particularly Mexican tradition—although it is widespread all through Latin America and wherever Hispanics live. It is always a part of the climax of *las posadas,* usually followed by *tamales* and hot chocolate, and *la misa de gallo.*

You can make your own *piñata* with a balloon, strips of newspaper for *papier maché,* paste, and colored paper. Inflate the balloon and paste several layers of newspaper over it. Let it dry thoroughly, possibly a day or longer. Repeat the process two more times, drying each application of paper thoroughly. Paint it in bright colors or add colored paper strips. Break the balloon, fill the cavity with candy, and seal the opening. Hang the *piñata* from a pole that can be raised and lowered in an attempt to confuse the blindfolded person who uses a stick or mallet to break it.

La piñata

Mexico

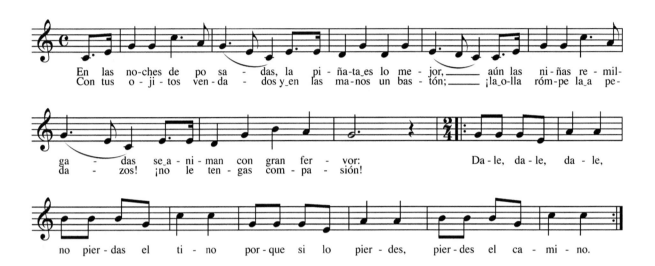

En las no-ches de po sa - das, la pi - ña-ta es lo me - jor, ___ aún las ni - ñas re - mil-
Con tus o - ji - tos ven - da - dos y en las ma-nos un bas - tón; ___ ¡la o-lla róm-pe la a pe-

ga - das se a - ni - man con gran fer - vor: Da - le, da - le, da - le,
da - zos! ¡no le ten - gas com - pa - sión!

no pier - das el ti - no por - que si lo pier - des, pier - des el ca - mi - no.

In the night of the *posadas* the piñata is the best; even the shyest girls are excited.
    Hit it, hit it, hit it, don't lose your aim, because if you lose it, you lose the path.

With your eyes blindfolded and a mallet in your hand, break the pot to pieces, have no compassion!
    Hit it, hit it, hit it, don't lose your aim, because if you lose it, you lose the path.

Other traditions unique to Mexico, particular to specific areas, include *la rama* in Vera Cruz where children decorate a branch, carry lanterns, and go from house to house begging *aguinaldos*. Another custom is *el viejo* in which university students dress outrageously as old men and old women and, carrying baby dolls, go from store to store for *aguinaldos*. There is *la noche de los rábanos*, night of the radishes, in Oaxaca in which craftsmen carve scenes on outsize radishes for competition and display in the *zócalo*. But above all, and quintessentially Mexican, are the feast of *la Virgen de Guadalupe*, *las posadas*, and *la piñata*.

New Mexico

Until now this book has dealt with countries of the Americas. Why now one of the fifty United States?

There are Hispanic populations throughout the country, especially in the larger cities and across the Southwest, but New Mexico is unique in that it is officially a bilingual state. Election ballots, examinations for drivers' licenses, official documents of various kinds, all must be printed in Spanish as well as English. Both languages—as well as a special kind of "Spanglish"—are heard on the streets and in shops. While most people of Hispanic background are today fluent in both languages, there remain some few among *los viejos* whose one language is Spanish, and almost all New Mexicans understand and speak a kind of "salt and pepper" English with Spanish words and phrases sprinkled in here and there.

As the language is retained, so are the traditions, the music, the food, the *farolitos* outlining every rooftop at Christmas time, much of the old culture, now liberally mixed with both Spanish and Mexican influences— Spanish largely in northern New Mexico, Mexican in the south—*río arriba* (upper) and *río abajo* (lower). Some say this imaginary line of separation occurs at Santa Fe. The river referred to is of course the Rio Grande.

Nevertheless there is very significant sameness in the two segments—the north and south, the Spanish and Mexican—in that they share the language, Roman Catholicism, the prevailing religion, the great love and protection of family and land, and the cultural heritage.

The Land and Its People

Archaeological remains identified as Sandia man lead to evidence of the first human life in New Mexico by about 25,000 BC. Between 10,000 and 8,000 BC hunters and gatherers, Clovis and Folsom peoples, occupied the land. Soon after that the first farmers, the Cochise, began cultivating corn, squash, and beans, still staples of the New Mexican diet.

By the beginning of the Christian Era, artistic pottery, weaving, and basketry were introduced by the Mogollon and Anasazi cultures. The Anasazi reached its high point of development in the Chaco civilization around 1200 AD, and Pueblo Indians had established villages along the Rio Grande by at least that time. The Navajo appeared on the New Mexico scene not before 1000, and possibly not in substantial numbers before 1500.

Today descendents of the Pueblo and Navajo Indians still live in the places their ancestors established.

Sixth most sparsely populated state in the nation, New Mexico is fifth largest in area. It is an arid land of mountains and deserts and plains. It is bisected north to south by the Rio Grande. Towering mountains in the north, the Sangre de Cristo and the Jemez, and southern ranges including Sacramento, Mogollon, Guadalupe, Organ, San Andres, and others, are the southernmost arms of the Rocky Mountains. New Mexico is bordered by Texas and Oklahoma on the east, Mexico on the south, Arizona on the west, Colorado on the north. At its northwest corner New Mexico joins Arizona, Utah, and Colorado to form the Four Corners, the only place in the United States where four states touch each other.

New Mexico has millions of acres of government-owned densely forested land with four national forests, Carson, Santa Fe, Lincoln, and Cíbola, as well as numerous other protected lands and monuments.

The population of New Mexico is almost two million, about 42% of whom are Hispanic and just over 10% Indian. This is the highest percentage of *hispanos* in any state and second highest percentage of Indians.

Although he may never have set foot in New Mexico, after a shipwreck Alvar Nuñuz Cabeza de Baca made his way along the Gulf of Mexico and into Texas before finally reaching Mexico. His tales of the journey between 1528 and 1536 created interest in exploring the land north of Mexico. The rumors of seven golden cities were sufficiently exciting that the viceroy of Mexico in 1539 sent Fr. Marcos de Niza, accompanied by Estevan, a Moor who had been Cabeza de Baca's companion, to find this fabled Cíbola.

History will likely never be able to tell the full story of the expedition, for de Niza's account differs from facts discovered later. We know for sure that Estevan was killed at Zuni and that de Niza's story of the cities of gold was false.

Trusting the friar's story, Francisco Vásquez de Coronado set out in 1540 with 335 Spaniards, 1300 Indians, four Franciscan friars including de Niza, on the most exciting treasure hunt in the New World's history. He found instead only simple dusty Indian villages. These, Hawikuh, home of the Zuni Indians, were de Niza's Cíbola, the cities of gold. The friar was sent back to Mexico in disgrace, and Coronado continued his journey.

They found no gold, but they were able to replenish their supplies to continue their journey, sometimes taking food from the natives by force, creating ill will along their way. With the onset of winter, Coronado set up camp in the Tiguex villages, near present-day Bernalillo, north of Albuquerque. Spanish confiscation of Indian goods led to the bloody Tiguex War in which the pueblos were destroyed and hundreds of Indians killed.

Coronado continued his search, now following advice of natives who persuaded him to go farther east where he would find a rich country called Quivira. Near present-day Wichita, Kansas, he did find a poor little pueblo with the name Quivira, but it was far from being the place of promised riches, and Coronado returned to New Mexico, eventually going back, dispirited, to Mexico.

There were four unsuccessful incursions in the 1580s and 1590s. In 1598 Don Juan de Oñate led his party of about 400 men, 130 of them with their wives and children, and several Franciscans to establish a colony just north of the pueblo Oke Owinge (formerly San Juan) where the Chama River joins the Rio Grande. They called the pueblo San Juan de los caballeros in honor of, according to Oñate's chronicler Gaspar Pérez de Villagra, "those noble sons who first raised in these barbarous regions the bloody tree upon which Christ perished for the redemption of mankind." The "noble sons" presumably were the priests and monks who had become martyrs during the various expeditions.

Coming prepared to stay, Oñate's party brought 83 wagons of supplies and equipment and some 7,000 head of livestock, including cattle, sheep, goats, colts and mares. Within a few months they moved their settlement from Oke Owinge to the west side of the river and established San Gabriel. These two became the first permanent European settlements in North America, beginning twenty-two years before the English Pilgrims landed in Massachusetts.

Santa Fe was founded, with Don Pedro de Peralta as New Mexico's first royal governor, in 1609-1610. It became then and remains today the capital city of New Mexico.

The seventeenth century was a difficult time as newcomers eked out their living in a harsh environment. Some of the natives were friendly and helpful, others deeply resentful of the Spaniards. The priests worked valiantly to convert the Indians who somehow managed to maintain their own religions while incorporating elements of Christianity.

But tensions built until in 1680 there erupted the well-planned Pueblo Revolt, led by Popé of San Juan and Taos, Catiti of Santo Domingo, Tupatú of Picuris, and Jaca of Taos. Twelve priests and some 375 settlers were killed, churches destroyed. Under the leadership of Governor Antonio de Otermín, the remaining settlers made their way south to the El Paso area. Twelve years later, 1692, Don Diego de Vargas successfully re-captured Santa Fe, and the settlers returned from their exile.

The eighteenth century brought an uneven, uneasy peace. More immigrating Spaniards and Mexicans arrived. Conversion attempts continued. The Pueblo Indians lived mostly in their small native villages, the Spaniards in their own villages. Now a new threat arose: Comanche and Navajo Indians regularly raided the villages of both groups, stealing food supplies, horses, even people. This recurring threat caused a somewhat tenuous alliance of Pueblo Indians and Spaniards for protection of the villages.

The most radical change came in the nineteenth century. Mexico—including New Mexico—became independent from Spain in 1821. Mexican citizenship was short lived however. In that same year Mexico announced a free-trade policy, and William Becknell, a trader from Missouri, was quick to be the first American to take advantage of the opportunity.

The Santa Fe Trail was operational in 1822. It immediately saw constant use by the Americans who were eager to sell their goods and by the Spaniards who were hungry for outside wares. This also brought a new group of immigrants, the Americans, referred to as "Anglos." To this day any New Mexican not of Indian or Hispanic heritage is called "Anglo," whether or not he has any trace of English background.

The Mexican War with the United States ended disastrously for Mexico, for it lost much of its northern territory. General Stephen Watts Kearny took possession of Santa Fe on August 18, 1846. The war ended in 1848, and on September 9, 1850, New Mexico was declared a territory of the United States. This area comprised present-day New Mexico, Arizona, parts of southern Colorado, southern Nevada, and southern Utah. In 1853 the territory was divided in half, the western portion becoming Arizona.

Citizens fought for statehood, but the land was "too Hispanic," "too Catholic," and the decision-makers of Washington did not like its name! But finally, on January 6, 1912, New Mexico became the forty-seventh state of the union.

The twentieth century saw much growth in the population and the advantageous development of a tri-cultural community in which diversity is recognized as a great strength.

Notable among twentieth century events was the influx to New Mexico of many artists—painters, sculptors, craftsmen, musicians, writers—drawn by the natural beauty of the state as well as by its cultural identity. Also notable was the installation of federal and state governmental institutions, possibly because of its relative isolation and its generally good weather. New Mexico has been a leader in nuclear, solar, and geothermal energy research and development. The Sandia National Laboratories and Kirtland Air Force Base have been prominent in nuclear research and special weapons development. The atomic bomb that ended World War II was developed at Los Alamos National Laboratory, founded as a part of the Manhattan Project in 1942. Environmental science, the search for alternate sources of energy, and various other scientific applications continue at LANL and the other New Mexico laboratories.

Art and science join ranching and agriculture as principal activities of today's New Mexicans as the three historic cultures have welcomed into their midst other groups, Asians, African-Americans, to become truly a multi-cultural state.

✳ Christmas Traditions

New Mexicans join with most Latin Americans in celebrating Christmas with *Las Posadas*, nativity scenes in homes and stores and churches, caroling from house to house, and festive family gatherings, but they also have some unique, or nearly unique, customs that reflect their tri-cultural life.

Lighting the Way

Nothing more clearly defines the Christmas season in New Mexico, nor more strikingly sets the scene for its dual sacred/secular nature, than its multitude of lights—*luminarias* and *farolitos*, the little fires that guide María and José during *las posadas*; *los pastores* as they make their way to Bethlehem; the villagers as they go to *la misa del gallo*; or the *abuelos* as they come down from the hills.

Luminarias traditionally have been medium-size bonfires built in a square of twigs and pitchy sticks of wood interlocked in log cabin style. In earlier times nearly every home burned a *luminaria* in its front yard, often on the nine nights preceding Christmas, definitely on *la Nochebuena*. They are less prominent now though they are still to be seen in village plazas and near the churches.

Farolitos (little lanterns) line rooftops, driveways, gates and fences, and every imaginable structure throughout New Mexico, creating an almost magical display of light and warmth on cold December nights. Unlike the stationary *luminarias*, *farolitos* are often carried in procession. A paper bag, a votive candle, and a firm bed of sand are the only ingredients needed for making your own *farolito*.

New Mexicans differ in naming these Christmas lights. *Norteños* (northern New Mexicans) distinguish between the bonfires and the little paper-bag lanterns, but others tend to call both kinds of lights *luminarias*.

Los Abuelos

Abuelos is a good word. It simply means grandfathers or grandparents, but in December, and especially in the mountain towns and villages of northern New Mexico, it takes on a different, sinister meaning.

"If you are not good, if you do not learn your prayers, the *abuelos* will come and take you away…" parents tell their children.

In the children's eyes, the *abuelos* are ugly, deformed, hairy, animal-like creatures who live in caves in the mountains. They are dressed in ragged clothes of deerskin or sheepskin. Their faces are painted grotesquely or they wear masks that inspire terror. They carry *chicotes* (whips) and sacks presumably to collect disobedient, careless children. Their voices are high and squeaky. The children hear them from afar as they come down the mountain, howling and cracking their whips. If there are *abuelas* (grandmothers) among the *abuelos*, they are actually men dressed as women.

Luminarias are built in the villages, one per night during the nine-day novena, to attract the *abuelos*. "*¿Donde están los muchachitooooos?*" (where are the little children) they call, and the children rush to hiding places. Older children stand near the luminarias and tease the *abuelos*, "*Abuelitos, vengan pa'ca,*" (Abuelitos, come here), and then they run when the *abuelos* respond.

The hiding places are soon discovered—under the bed, in the closet, behind a door—and the *abuelos* continue their reign of terror, cracking their whips and screaming at the children to say their prayers or to dance *La Palomita* (an old Spanish folkdance).

The *abuelos* will always ask the children if they have learned their prayers. If the children have been well-taught by their parents, they are able to recite *Oremos*:

> *Oremos, oremos,*
> *angelitos somos;*
> *del cielo venemos,*
> *a pedir oremos*
> *y si no nos den oremos*
> *puertas y ventanas*
> *quebraremos.*

> > (Let us pray, let us pray, we are little angels, we come from heaven to beg *oremos*—in earlier times the word *aguinaldos* was used in place of *oremos* here—and if you don't give us *oremos*, we will break your doors and windows.)

These time-honored traditions, older than anyone can guess, are still practiced, though they are not so widespread as they once were. Through the years they served as a means to teach prayers, songs and dances, and the culture of the village and the people.

Finally the *abuelos* fill their sacks not with captured children but with *empanadas* and other good foods of the season and return to their secret places until next year. The younger children, duly impressed, hurry to bed, safe in the assurance they have escaped the wrath of the *abuelos* for another year. Older children now take their own sacks and go to the houses displaying *luminarias*, reciting *Oremos, oremos,* or a shortcut, *mis crismas* (my Christmas treats), to collect candy, fruit, and other treats, to share *abrazos*, and to warm up by the *fogón* (hearth) with a cup of hot cocoa before continuing their journey.

Los animales hablaron

The animals spoke on the first Christmas Eve. The cow (*la vaca*) had nothing to say at first, but she warmed the holy Child with her breath. *El gallo* (the rooster) crowed lustily, "*Cristo nació-ó-ó-ó-ó*" (Christ is born). *El caballo* (the horse) asked, "*¿Donde na-ci-ó-ó-ó-ó?*" (Where was he born?). *El borrego* (the sheep) answered, "*En Be-é-lé-é-é-n*" (in Bethlehem). Excited into action by her stable-mates' enthusiasm, *la vaca* now added, "*Vamos a ver*" (let's go see), and *el burro* (the donkey) said, "*lo es me-e-e-e-nester*" (it is what we should do).

Dando los días

In some villages on January 1 there occurs a daylong event in honor of all those named Manuel or Manuela. Immediately after midnight on this day, a group of musicians—singers, guitarists, violinists—gather and begin to go house to house to waken and to serenade the honoree on his saint's day. Often the songs and verses are improvised on the spot, but some are traditional, varying from community to community, with formulaic verses for approaching the house, standing outside the door, entering the house, and leaving. Not surprisingly, the "surprised" host has a *banquete* prepared, a table of food and drink, perhaps a small gift of money for the musicians. Singing and dancing occur throughout the day at the church, in the plaza, at various homes where the *Manueles,* their families and friends celebrate with good food and good humor.

Autos Sacramentales

Autos sacramentales are acts or ordinances pertaining to sacraments, or simply acts of faith. Religious drama was popular throughout medieval Europe. In England there was the morality play, in Spain the *auto sacramental*. The oldest known *auto* was *El auto de los Reyes Magos*, performed in about 1150 in the Cathedral of Toledo.

It is not surprising that these dramas came to the New World with the first Christians, nor is it surprising that they were used as teaching tools to convert the Indians.

New Mexico has at least six extant *autos sacramentales*, three of them related to Christmas, *Los Pastores*, *Los Tres Reyes Magos*, and *Los Comanchitos*.

Los Pastores

Pastorelas (shepherds' plays), developed from the *autos*, were specifically portrayals of the shepherds on the night of the birth of Jesus. The earliest known version of *Los Pastores* was written in Spain in 1612 by Lope de Vega. In one of its many variations, it is performed regularly in villages and towns across the state. Some forty versions, both words and music, are said to exist in New Mexico, many of them handed down orally from generation to generation.

As the play begins, we find a number of shepherds resting when one of them, Tubal, bursts excitedly into their midst to tell of the archangel Michael's news of the birth of Jesus and that they all should go to Bethlehem to worship him. The shepherds, Bato, lazy Bartolo, the Hermit, and others begin to make immediate plans for the gifts they would take to the Baby—a woolen wrap, a pillow, a little hat, a flower. Gila, the gentle shepherdess, makes sure there are plenty of *tamales* for the journey. Before they go, however, they must rest a little. As they sleep, Lucifer (Satan) comes to the

Hermit and, in an effort to thwart the shepherds' plans, tries to convince him to seduce Gila and flee with her. The others wake up, Michael re-appears, and a fierce battle ensues between the archangel and Lucifer. Lucifer is defeated, and the shepherds make their way to Bethlehem.

Following are songs from various enactments of *Los Pastores*.

New Mexico

Es - ta no - che con la lu - na, y ma-ña - na con el sol, ca - mi - ne - mos con con - ten - to a ver a_es te Re - den - tor.

Tonight with the moon and tomorrow with the sun, let us travel happily to see this Redeemer.

Her - ma-nos pas - to - res, her - ma-nos que - ri - dos, va - mos tran - si - tan - do por es - tos ca - mi - nos.

Brother shepherds, beloved brothers, let's travel through these pathways.

New Mexico

De la real Je - ru - sa - lén sa - le_u - na_es - tre - lla bri - llan - do que_a los pas - to - res va gui - an - do pa - ra el por - tal de Be - lén.

From royal Jerusalem there shines a brilliant star that guides the shepherds to the stable at Bethlehem.

Va mos ca - mi - nan do con mu cho con - ten - to a_a do rar al Ni ño en su na - ci - mien to.

We are traveling happily to adore the Child in his birthplace.

Duer - me - te ni - ño lin - do___ en los bra - zos del__ a - mor,___ mien - tras que duer me_y des-

can - sa la pe - na de mi do lor. A la ru, ___ a la me, __ a la ru, a la me. A la

ru, ___ a la me, ___ a la ru, a la ru, a la me. ___

Sleep beautiful child in the arms of love; while you sleep the pain of my sorrow sleeps and rests.

Goodbye Joseph, Goodbye Mary, goodbye dear little child,
now the shepherds are leaving for the fields of Egypt.

Los Tres Magos

Los Tres Magos is a much shorter *auto*. It is performed on the day of the Three Kings, January 6. This re-enactment of the Wise Men's visit to the Baby Jesus includes a visit to King Herod in which the King asks them to come back to tell him where to find the Child. They choose to go home by a different route, however, for they suspect King Herod is up to no good. It is after this that Herod orders that all baby boys be slaughtered to make sure his own power is not threatened by the newborn Holy Child. This precipitates the flight to Egypt by the Holy Family.

Los Comanchitos

     Los Comanchitos, unlike *Los Pastores* and *Los Tres Magos*, a folk drama associated with the Christmas season, has no previous association with Spain, but rather is a pure product of New Mexico and its troubled history with the Comanche Indians.

     After the re-conquest in 1692-1693, the Pueblo Indians adapted their own religious beliefs to those of the *hispanos*, finding ways to keep the two separate without compromising their own integrity. This satisfied a main goal of the missionaries, and Puebloans and settlers were able to live together in reasonably peaceful conditions.

     Not so with the Navajo and Comanches. These groups—hunters, nomads—had never lived in established communities as the Pueblo Indians had for centuries, and their life was very different. Because of their frequent raids on the pueblos and villages, they acquired a reputation for thievery and kidnapping. *Los Comanchitos* is a light-hearted take on this reputation.

     As it is sometimes seen today, the Comanches are looking for *el Santo Niño*, stopping at several houses before they find him. A prayer vigil is going on, and the Comanches are invited to enter. They participate by dancing for the Baby, but slyly, they are watching for a chance to steal the Child and escape. The others chase the kidnappers. When they catch the Comanches, they arrange ransom for the Child by promising to host the party next year.

     Another version combines elements of *Los Tres Magos* and *Los Comanches* in which the Comanches interrupt the adoration and gift-giving of the Wise Men, steal the Baby and escape.

Los Matachines

Perhaps the most spectacular of all New Mexican dance dramas is *Los Matachines,* performed on saints days and at Christmas by *hispanos* in villages like Alcalde, El Rancho, Arroyo Seco, and by Indians in Jemez, Taos, San Ildefonso, Oke Owinge, and other pueblos.

Sixteenth century dance historian Thoinot Arbeau wrote in *Orchesography* of a sword dance called *Mattachins* or *Bouffons.* Medieval masked dances—*Matacinioo* in Italy, *Matachins* in France, and *Matachini* in Spain—bear sufficient resemblance to today's New Mexico *matachines* that direct lineage can be assumed. The European dancers are described as masked jesters who wore brightly colored ribbons hanging from their shoulders, bells on their legs, and helmet-like headdresses.

It is less difficult to accept this as the history of the *matachines* than to understand how the dance has survived in a fairly consistent pattern through centuries of semi-isolation in New Mexico where only the memory of *los viejos* kept it alive. Here, however, it has taken on a religious meaning, leaving little room for the jesters..

Principal figures are *el Monarca* (the king) and *la Malinche,* a young girl and the only female in the dance, a symbol of innocence and purity. She is dressed all in white, complete with white gloves and veil, and carries only a silk handkerchief.

There usually are twelve *matachín* dancers all of whom wear dark trousers, coat, and gloves with bright ribbons streaming down their backs. Their headdress, called *cupil,* shaped somewhat like a bishop's mitre, is attached to a long colorful cape. Masks cover the lower half of their faces, and a strip of fringe hangs from the front of the *cupil* falling over their eyes. Each *matachin* carries a trident (*palma*) in one hand and a gourd rattle in the other.

The *matachines* face each other in two lines. *El Monarca* often dances between the lines or leads one line, then the other. The dance is in simple steps but intricate patterns. The lines meet and return, cross over, make figure eights and serpentine lines, and other complex designs, all in careful precision.

Other characters are one or more *abuelos* who are masked and roughly dressed. They carry whips they don't hesitate to use to capture the attention of onlookers. They direct dancers to their places, adjust ribbons and other parts of the dancers' dress, and they actively participate as dancers with *la Malinche* and *el toro* (the bull).

El toro is usually a young boy. He wears an animal skin with a headdress of horns. He walks leaning over two sticks, pretending to walk like an animal. He interacts with the *matachines* and is perhaps the symbol of evil. He is eventually symbolically killed.

The music, played almost always on violins and guitars, is highly repetitive, played over and over, sometimes dozens of times. There is much sameness to the tunes, but of course they are not identical from venue to venue.

The tunes here, taken from *The Matachines Dance of the Upper Rio Grande, History,* by Flavia Waters Champe, were collected between the 1940s and 1970s in the pueblo of San Ildefonso. They are representative of some of the dance tunes heard in many versions of *Los Matachines*.

Opening dance of el Monarca and the Matachines

Malinche's dance before el Monarca

el Toro and el Monarca

el Monarca wheels in groups of three, with each couple

the performers leave the dance area

The Music

Villancicos

In the fourteenth century the word *villancico* referred to a song or poem inspired by the songs and dances of *los campesinos* (the country people, peasants) or *los villanos* (the villagers), those who lived in the villages as opposed to the more sophisticated city-dwellers. In his *Tesoro de la lengua castellana o español* of 1611, however, the lexicographer Sebastián de Covarrubias indicated that the *villancico* was only an *imitación* of the songs sung by *campesinos*, a stylized version rather than the actual music that arose from the folk. This definition was upheld in the 1739 *Diccionario de autoridades*, a precursor to *El Diccionario de la Real Academia Española*.

The *villancico* was at first a simple, secular tune with popular and dramatic roots, probably evolving from the medieval Arabic *zajel* (a type of mystical poetry). Its two-part form was known as "head" and "feet," the "head" being the *estribillo* (refrain), the "feet" being *versos* or *coplas* (stanzas). The *coplas* were related to the *estribillo* in their themes. The word always dominated, the musical setting simply enhancing the text. This created a great rhythmic freedom in the *coplas*, similar to the recitative in opera. Often soloists sang the *coplas* and a chorus sang the *estribillo*.

Gradually the *villancico* came to be religious in nature, at first extolling the saints and special feast days of the church; eventually it became almost always associated with Christmas. The most famous Spanish collection of *villancicos* is the *Cancionero de Palacio*, published in 1500.

By 1539 the *villancico* was noted in New Spain. It was clearly religious and definitely used to convert the Indians. The religious aspects, however, were mixed with dramatic parody where various segments of the populations—Blacks, Indians, Roman Catholic clergy—were caricatured, using speech patterns and dialects that reflected the groups. Sor Juana Inés de la Cruz was famous in the New World for writing *villancico* poems that were obviously parodies while they still maintained a spirit of reverence.

In the Americas there came to be in the *villancicos* more regular meter, making it easier to translate the songs and to add rhythms native to the different groups of people. Secular themes began to be mixed with religious themes. The tunes remained simple with obvious harmonic structure; parallel thirds became prominent elements. There were syncopation and triplets from the various native rhythms. By the end of the seventeenth century *villancicos* were becoming *aguinaldos*.

Aguinaldos

Some put forth an interesting possibility for the derivation of the word *aguinaldos* and a strong connection with the winter solstice and Druidism. *Au-gui*, they say, is mistletoe from an evergreen tree, searched for by the druid priests who shared it as a precious gift, a means of salvation, with believers and followers of the Edda, the Druids' bible.

Aguinaldos began in Spain, particularly in Andalucía, where groups of young singers gathered to go in processions such as *las posadas* in which the Holy Family portray their journey to Bethlehem. The custom came early to the Americas, especially to Puerto Rico where it became a *trulla* (crowd) in which more and more people joined the singers and instrumentalists, all finally ending in an *asalto* (assault) where a pre-designated host had planned a party for all.

Today in South America the term *villancico* is more often used; in Central America and much of Mexico it's *aguinaldo*. Both are words for Christmas carol. There is another and well-known meaning for *aguinaldo* however. Many use the term to signify Christmas gifts, usually small gifts, often candy or liquor or cash, for those who have been helpful to them in business or in personal relations—employees, the postman, a teacher—or even small, loving gifts within the family. The idea of the *aguinaldo* is to show affection rather than ostentation. In some places the children beg *aguinaldos* as they would ask for "trick or treat" surprises, and they are usually rewarded with candy or other sweet treats. In New Mexico this practice corresponds to *mis crismas*.

The Songs

antos, tonadas, canciones are all Spanish-language words for our single word *song*. *Tonada* and *canción* seem to be roughly synonymous, with *canto* having a somewhat more specialized meaning, to be used with specific activities or events. *Cantos* are often associated with various occupations, with funerals, or with fiestas for example. Of course there are also different regional and national uses of all three words. For the most part, *canción* serves our purpose. It can be, as defined above, a *villancico*, an *aguinaldo*, or simply a *canción*.

Another special song is the *gaita*, native to Venezuela. The *gaita zuliana* is particularly prominent in the Caribbean region where native Indian elements combined with Spanish and African elements to create this form near the end of the eighteenth century. At first the *gaita* was a song of protest, but it has evolved into a larger repertoire, including Christmas themes.

The songs here are tied as much as possible to specific countries. I was unable to find a song unique to Paraguay, Guatemala, Honduras, Panamá or El Salvador. Most of the songs, however, are known and sung in those countries as well as in the rest of the area. When a song is given no country designation, it is one of general knowledge throughout the Spanish-speaking regions and is listed under the category *De Todas Partes* (from everywhere).

Most of the songs are presented without accompaniment, but chords for guitar or piano are included except for the few that seem to need no accompaniment other than perhaps a drum pattern or other percussive sound.

Two features typical of Spanish language songs should be noted: frequent elisions in which one syllable is tied to the next, both sung on the same pitch; and an accent "misplaced" by the rhythm of the melody, producing syncopation. Another rhythmic/melodic feature found often in

Spanish music is the *hemiola*, in which two measures notated in triple meter are sung or played as if they were in duple meter.

Many of the songs have strong ties to Spain, while others are native to countries in the western hemisphere. Literal translations are given for all the songs. Singable translations are not provided. In only one case— "Cascabel" (Jingle Bells)— have English words been translated, or adapted, into Spanish. This song was given to me by a woman from Nicaragua who cited it as a very popular song in her country in the form included here. Usually, the best one can do is adapt the meaning of the words, the sense of the song, to the rhythm of the melody, but in every case it is preferable to sing the song in its own language.

Most are folk tunes with no recognized composer, often with not even a real title, being named simply by the first few words of the text. The tunes range from simple *canciones infantiles* (childhood songs) to songs with complex rhythms. Some present a challenge, melodically and rhythmically.

Songs for *Las Posadas*, the breaking of the *piñata*, *Los Pastores*, and *Los Matachines* are so specific that they are included within the description of the events in earlier sections on Mexico and New Mexico respectively.

The Caribbean Islands

Cuba

   Ursula ¿que estás haciendo?

Dominican Republic

   Venid pastorcillos

Puerto Rico

   Felices pascuas
   Gloria a Dios

Ursula, ¿qué estás haciendo?

Cuba

1. Ursula, what are you doing spending so much time in the kitchen?
Mama, I am plucking the feathers from the chicken.
Oh how I like the *buñuelitos,* the hot bread, and the *asedito.*

2. Tonight is Nochebuena, night for making buñuelos,
in my house they aren't made for lack of flour and eggs.
How I love the *pastelitos*, the hot bread, and the good wine.

Venid pastorcillos

Dominican Republic

Come sheperds, come to worship the King of the heavens who is now born,
don't be afraid to come without rich offerings, the Baby is pleased with your faith and good will.
We are going happily to Bethlehem where the Son of Mary has been born. Jesus waits for us.
We will bring sweets and honey to offer the Baby Emanuel. Let us go to see the Baby Jesus.

Felices Pascuas

Puerto Rico
arranged by James and Isabel Carley

Merry Christmas ladies and gentlemen, now let us sing of the birth of the Son of God.

This song and Gloria a Dios are extremely effective with no other accompaniment than the hand drum patterns.

Gloria a Dios

Puerto Rico
arranged by James and Isabel Carley

"Glory to God in the highest," the angels sang, announcing to the shepherds that Jesus Christ had been born. Let's go, shepherds, let's go to worship the King of the heavens who has been born.

South America

Argentina

Adios año viejo
Aguinaldo de Lara
Al Niño recién nacido
En Belén
En el portal de Belén
Que lindo es el Niñito
Los Reyes Magos
Tres palomitas
Vamos pastorcillos
La Virgen María
Ya llegó la Nochebuena
Ya vienen los Reyes

Bolivia

Ama Niñito
Navidava puri nuhua

Chile

Arrú, arrú
Ha nacido en un portal
El Niño hermoso
Señora Dona María

Colombia

Tutaina
Vamos pastorcitos
Velo que bonito
Ven, ven, ven

Ecuador

Tun tun
Yo soy indiecito

Paraguay

See *De Todas Partes Perú*

Alegría en Navidad
Al huachi torito
Belenpis Huaccachcan
Huaccacuspansi
Niño Diosmi paccarimum
Vamos pastorcillos

Uruguay

Los pastores de Belén
Ya viene la vaca

Venezuela

Adorar al Niño
Aguinaldo
Niño lindo
Villancico

Adiós año viejo

Argentina

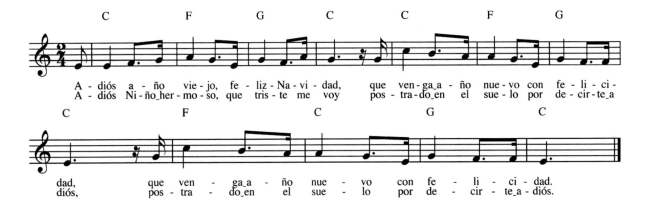

A - diós a - ño vie - jo, fe - liz - Na - vi - dad, que ven - ga_a - ño nue - vo con fe - li - ci -
A - diós Ni - ño_her - mo - so, que tris - te me voy pos - tra - do_en el sue - lo por de - cir - te_a

dad, que ven - ga_a - ño nue - vo con fe - li - ci - dad.
diós, pos - tra - do_en el sue - lo por de - cir - te_a - diós.

Goodbye old year, happy Christmas,
may the new year come with happiness.

Goodbye lovely Child, how sadly I leave
prostrate on the ground at telling you goodbye.

Aguinaldo de Lara

Argentina

Let us go to Bethlehem for there is much to see,
San José and the Virgin, San José and the Virgin,
the mule and the ox, San José and the Virgin, the mule and the ox.
New aguinaldos I bring you, new aguinaldos I bring you
from those that were sung to the Child and the Kings.

Al Niño recién nacido

Argentina

1. All offer a gift to the Child.
I am poor, I have nothing,
I offer him my heart.
   Huachito little bull from the corral.

2. From the tree was born the branch,
From the branch was born the flower,
From the flower was born María,
and from Mará was born the Lord.
   Huachito little bull from the corral.

En Belén

Argentina

En   Be - lén a - ca - ba   de na - cer mi bien;
Bai - len pas - tor ci - llos, bai - len o - tra vez,

va - mos pas - tor - ci - llos, va - mos a Be - lén.
que Je - sús na - ció   pa - ra nues - tro bien.

1. In Bethlehem my good fortune has just been born;
let's go, shepherds, let's go to Bethlehem.

2. Dance shepherds, dance again,
for Jesus is born for our benefit.

En el portal de Belén

Argentina

En el por-tal de Be - lén___ hay una ar - ca chi-qui - ti - ta don-de se viste_el Se - ñor___ pa-ra

sa - lir de vi - si - ta. Bai - lad, pas tor ci llos, bai - lad en Be lén, que Dios es na ci do pa - ra nues tro bien.

1. In the stable of Bethlehem there is a little ark where the Lord gets dressed to go visiting.
Dance little shepherds, dance in Bethlehem, for God has been born for our benefit.

2. En el portal de Belén hay piedra redonda, donde se sube el Señor para subir a la gloria.
Bailad, pastorcillos, bailad en Belén, que Dios es nacido para nuestro bien.

In the stable of Bethlehem there is a round rock where the Lord climbs to glory.

3. En el portal de Belén hay un espejo cuadrado, donde se mire el Señor con la Virgen a su lado.

In the stable of Bethlehem there is a square mirror where the Lord sees himself with the Virgin at his side.

4. Campanillas de Belén a la madruga suenan para al despertar al Niño que ha nacido en Nochebuena.

Little bells of Bethlehem ring at dawn to awaken the Child who was born on Christmas Eve.

5. En el portal de Belén gitanitos han entrado y al niñito de María los pañales le han robado.
In the stable of Bethlehem gypsies have entered and have stolen the diapers of the Child of María.

6. En el portal de Belén hay estrellas, sol y luna, la Virgen y San José y el Niño que está en la cuna.

In the stable of Bethlehem there are stars, sun and moon, the Virgin and San José, and the Child in the cradle.

Que lindo es el Niñito

Argentina

1. How beautiful is the Child, I would die for Him.
His little face enchants me, his eyes also.
Because the eternal Father with his great power
wanted the Child to be beautiful as He is,
The Virgin sings to him, also San José,
Let us sing too.

2. How beautiful is the grape in the vineyard,
more beautiful is the Child on the altar.
Oh my beautiful child, O my immortal God,
you have been born humbly in this stable.
The Virgin sings to him, also San José,
Let us sing too.

Los Reyes Magos

Argentina

Through mountains of sand, to the edges of the sea
the three Wise Kings have just arrived.
First Melchior, second Gaspar, and the darkest one the King Balthasar.

Tres palomitas

Argentina

Tres pa - lo - mi - tas, en un pa - lo - mar   su - ben y   ba - jan al   pie del al - tar.
To - can la   mi - sa, le - van - tan la   voz,   be - san y   be - san la   ma - no de   Dios.

Por a - quel pos - ti - go   a - bier - to se   pa - sea u-na   don - ce - lla,   se   pa - se - a.____
Ves - ti - da   de a zul   y   blan - co, her - mo - sa   co - mo   es - tre - lla,   co-mo es   tre - lla.____

1. Three little doves in a dovecote flying up and down at the foot of the altar :‖
Through the open shutter a maiden passes :‖

2. They play the mass, they raise their voice, kissing and kissing the hand of God :‖
Dressed in blue and white, beautiful as a star :‖

Vamos pastorcillos

Argentina

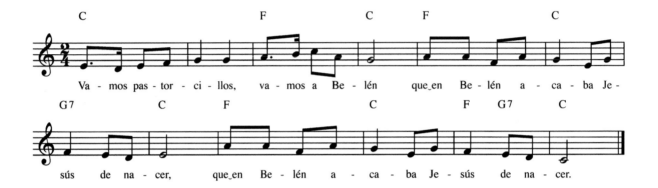

Va - mos pas - tor - ci - llos, va - mos a Be - lén que_en Be - lén a - ca - ba Je - sús de na - cer, que_en Be - lén a - ca - ba Je - sús de na - cer.

Let's go shepherds, let's go to Bethlehem
for in Bethlehem Jesus has just been born.

La Virgen María

Argentina

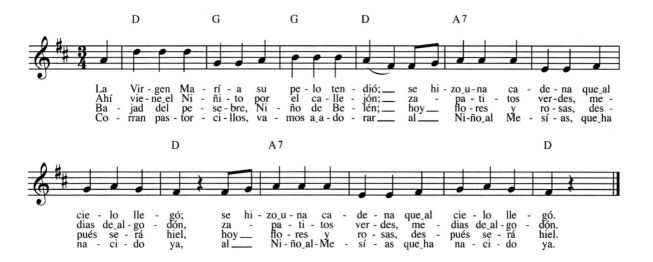

La Vir - gen Ma - rí - a su pe - lo ten - dió;___ se hi - zo_u - na ca - de - na que_al
Ahí vie - ne_el Ni - ñi - to por el ca - lle - jón;___ za - pa - ti - tos ver - des, me -
Ba - jad del pe - se - bre, Ni - ño de Be - lén;___ hoy___ flo - res y ro - sas, des -
Co - rran pas - tor - ci - llos, va - mos a_a - do - rar___ al___ Ni - ño_al Me - sí - as, que_ha

cie - lo lle - gó; se hi - zo_u - na ca - de - na que_al cie - lo lle - gó.
dias de_al - go - dón, za - pa - ti - tos ver - des, me - dias de_al - go - dón.
pués se - rá hiel, hoy___ flo - res y ro - sas, des - pués se - rá hiel.
na - ci - do ya, al___ Ni - ño_al - Me - sí - as que_ha na - ci - do ya.

1. The Virgin María tended to her hair, a chain that reached heaven.

2. There comes the Child through the alley, little green shoes, cotton hose.

3. Down from the stable, Child of Bethlehem; today flowers and roses, later bitterness.

4. Run shepherds, let's go to worship the Child, the Messiah who is born.

Ya llegó la Nochebuena

Argentina

Ya lle - gó la No - che - bue - na, ya lle - gó la Na - vi - dad. Can - ta - re - mos a - la -
ban - zas pa - ra el Ni - ño que ven - drá. Va mos to - dos a es pe - rar - lo, va mos to - dos a Be -
lén, que Je - sús en un pe - se - bre pa - ra to - dos va a na - cer.

Christmas Eve has arrived, Christmas is here.
Let us sing songs of praise for the Child who will come.
Let's all go to await him, let's all go to Bethlehem,
for Jesus is born in a manger for all of us.

Ya vienen los Reyes

Argentina

Estribillo:
Here come the Kings through the oak woods,
Melchior goes ahead, Gaspar follows, and last of all goes the great Balthasar.

1. The Wise Kings travel on the road to Bethlehem,
the snow covers the path, the star serves as guide.

2. Balthasar brought him gold, Gaspar carries honey, Melchior richest incense,
and a shepherd girl a carnation for her King.

3. Jesus didn't look at the gold but he looked at the carnation,
the Virgin with a little finger put honey on his lips.

4. The shepherds and the Kings went together to worship Him,
the Kings soon left, but the shepherds remained.

Ama Niñito

(Don't cry, Baby Jesus)

Bolivia

A - ma ni - ñi - to wa - gay chu ma - may - qui nu - ne___ chi - son ya.

Hum___

Navidava puri nuhua

Bolivia

Na - vi - da - va   pu - ri - ni - hua,   hua - hua - no - ka   ku - si - chu   ña - my,   Ni - ño Je -
La Na - vi - dad   ha lle - ga - do,   hi - jos, nos   al - le - gra - re - mos___   por - que al

sús yu - ryt lay - cu   a - na - ta - ña la - kis - ka -   Ji - cha ka   tus - ta - na - kam -
Ni - ño Je - sús   le va   a gus tar   ju - gar con sus___   Va - mos a -   do - rar lo, va -

py,   Be - len - a   ru - sa ra - ña - ni.   Ji - cha ka   ni   Jua - ua - na - ca.
mos, va - mos a - do - rar - lo, va - mos.   Va mos a - lli,   hi - jos va - mos.

Christmas has come, children,
Let us rejoice because the Child Jesus will enjoy playing with his children.
Let's go to worship him,
Let's go, let's go to worship Him.
Let's go there, children let's go.

Arrú arrú

Chile

1. Arrú, arrú my Child, arrú arrú without equal
little eyes of light, little mouth of coral.

2. We go quickly there to present ourselves
to this tender Child who comes today to save us.

3. Give us my Child your blessing
so that we may receive pardon from God.

Ha nacido en un portal

Chile

He has been born in a stall, filled with spider webs,
between the mule and the ox. The Redeemer of souls.
Lovely little Baby, come here,
your beautiful eyes will save me
because the Virgin María has carried me to the heavens.

El Niño hermoso

Cuan do la Vir gen Ma - rí - a___ Dió_a luz el Ni-ño de Dios___

Tan her mo-so que na - ció___ que_el mun-do cau-so_ar-mo - ní - a.___

When the Virgin María gave birth to the Child of God,
He was so beautiful that he brought harmony to the world.

Señora Dona María

Chile

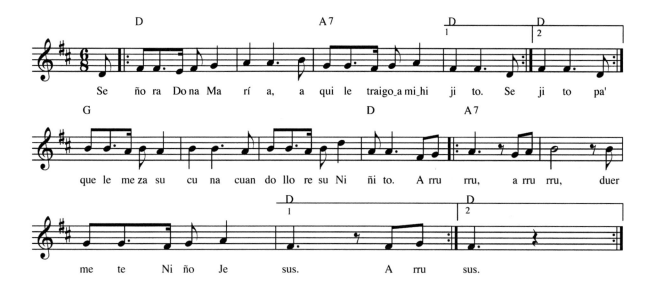

Se ño ra Do na Ma rí a, a qui le traigo a mi hi ji to. Se ji to pa'

que le me za su cu na cuan do llo re su Ni ñi to. A rru rru, a rru rru, duer

me te Ni ño Je sus. A rru sus.

Lady María, I bring my little child here
so that you rock his cradle when your baby cries.
Hush, hush, sleep Baby Jesus.

Tutaina

Colombia

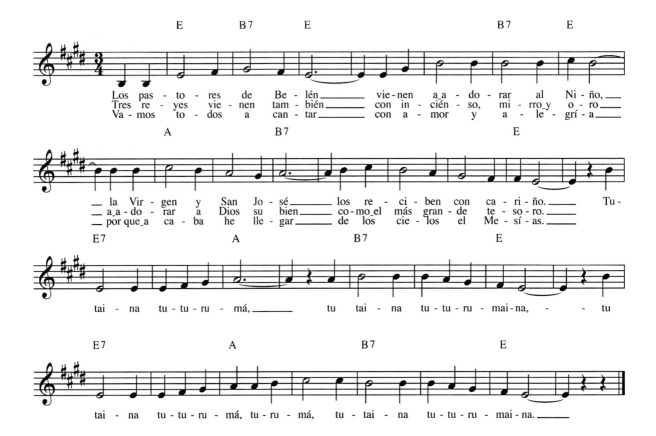

The shepherds of Bethlehem are coming to worship the Child,
the Virgin and Saint Joseph receive them with warmth.

Three kings come also with incense, myrrh and gold
to worship God their beloved as the greatest treasure.

Let's all go to sing with love and happiness
because the Messiah has just come from the heavens.

Vamos Pastorcitos

Colombia

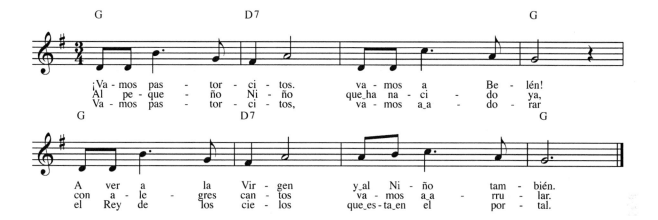

¡Va - mos pas - tor - ci - tos. va - mos a Be - lén!
Al pe - que - ño Ni - ño que_ha na - ci - do ya,
Va - mos pas - tor - ci - tos, va - mos a_a - do - rar

A ver a la Vir - gen y_al Ni - ño tam - bién.
con a - le - gres can - tos va - mos a_a - rru - lar.
el Rey de los cie - los que_es - ta_en el por - tal.

1. Let's go, shepherds, let's go to Bethlehem
to see the Virgin and the Child also.

2. We are going to sing happy songs
to the little newborn Child.

3. Let's go, shepherds, let's go to worship
the King of the heavens who is in the stable.

Velo que bonito

Traditional Colombia (Pacifico)
Arranged by Pilar Posada

Velo que bo-ni-to lo vie-nen ba-jan-do con ra-mos de flo-res lo van a-dor-nan-do.

Que bo-ni-to él ba-jó, con flo - res se_a-dor-nó.

U - - rrí, u - rrá, San An - to-nio ya se va.

U-rru rru rru-rrí, u-rru-rra, es que San An-to-nio ya se va.

Se-ño-ra San-ta na por-qué llo-ra_el ni-ño, San An - to-nio ya se va.
Por u-na man-za-na que se le_ha per-di-do San An - to-nio ya se va.

El ni-ño_es-tá, es-tá llo-ran-do y San An-to-nio ya se va.
Se le per-dió u-na man-za-na

U - - rrí, u - rrá, San An - to-nio ya se va.

U-rru rru rru-rrí, u-rru-rrá, es que San An-to-nio ya se va.

See how beautifully they are coming down, adorning him with branches of flowers.
Hush, hush, St. Anthony is leaving.
Señora Santa Anna, why is the child crying? St. Anthony is passing by.
For an apple he has lost, St. Anthony is leaving.

Ven, ven, ven

Colombia

Ven, ven, ven, que ya la fies - ta va_a_em pe - zar, ven, ven, ven que_al Ni - ño Dios __ __ hay que can - tar. No - che - bue - na, no - che de paz, co - mo_a lum - - bran las es - tre - llas pe - ro la lu - na_a - lum - bra más.

Come, come, come, for the fiesta is about to begin,
come, come, come, we must sing for the Baby Jesus.
Christmas Eve, night of peace,
the stars shine, but the moon shines more.

Tun tun

Ecuador

Tun tun ¿Quién es? Gen-te de paz, __ á - bra nos la puer ta __ que __ ya_es Na-vi-

dad. Tun tun ¿Quién es? Gen-te de paz, __ a - bra nos la puer - ta __ que __

_ ya_es Na-vi - - - dad. Que ven - ga_el co mi - sa - rio pre - mi - ro_a ve-ri-

guar __ si son __ per - so-nas de_or - den, o quie - ren per-tu - bar.

Knock knock. Who is it? People of peace,
0pen the door for it is Christmas.
The comissioner will come first to investigate
if you are orderly people or those who cause trouble.

2. Tun tun....
Si es que ha nacido el Niño, pues, váyanse a Belén,
que yo desde mi cama les doy mi parabién.
    If the Child has been born, then go on to Bethlehem; from my bed I give you my congratulations.

3. Tun tun....
Me están robando el sueño, me arruinan la salud;
no quiero transnocharme, porque nació Jesús.
    You are robbing my sleep, ruining my health; I don't want to spend a sleepless night because Jesus
    is born.

4. Tun tun....
No quiero abrir mi puerta, molestan más allá,
que el diablo se los lleve, a mi déjenme en paz.
    I don't want to open my door, you are bothering me, let the devil take you, and leave me in peace.

This song, similar to those in the *las posadas* drama, is sung in Ecuador, Venezuela, and other South
American countries. It is a dialogue between the innkeeper and the travelers seeking lodging.

Yo soy indiecito

Ecuador

Yo soy in - die - ci - to de San Se - bas - tián, de San Se - bas - tián.

En a - yu - nas ven - go y sin al - mor - zar, y sin al - mor - zar, por

cum - plir la vi - gi - lia de la Na - vi - dad, de la Na - vi - dad.

I'm a little Indian from San Sebastian, and I have been fasting since the early morn,
all for to fulfill my vigil now that Christ is born.

Alegría en Navidad

Perú

So - pa le die-ran al Ni - ño, no se la qui-so co - mer, _____ y co mo_es ta - ba tan
dul - ce, se la co mió San Jo - sé. _____ Va-mos al por - tal, con su res plan - dor,
que sal-ga la lu-na lle-na y el_her mo-so sol, e - llos nos a lum-bra-rán con su res-plan dor.
A - le-grí-a, a - le-grí-a, a - le-grí-a y pla cer, es ta no-che næce_el Ni-ño en el por tal de Be lén.

They gave food to the Child, he did not want to eat it
and since it was so sweet, San José ate it.
Let's go to the stable with its radiance,
let the moon and the sun come out and illuminate us with their radiance.
Joy, joy, joy and pleasure, this night the Child is born in the stable of Bethlehem.

Al huachi torito

Perú, Argentina

All offer a gift to the newborn Child. I am poor, I have nothing, I offer him my heart.
Huachi, huachi, little bull from the corral.
Raise your eyes to heaven and you will see the Baby God dressed in white linen giving you his blessing.
From the trunk is born the branch, from the branch the flower, from the flower María was born, and
from María the Redeemer.
Good evening my little Child, I have come to visit you, this day the 24th, the eve of Christmas.

Belenpis Huaccachcan
Villancico de Huamanga

Perú

Be - len - pis hua - ccach - can sú - macc Ni-ño - cha. Hi - na - ya hua - cca - chun hu -
Di - cen que en Be-lén llo - ran-do es-tá el Ni ño. De - jen que llo - re, mis pe - ca -

chai - ta mai - llan. Sa - ccey sa - ccey hi - na hua ccacc - ta pai - pa hue - ccen-cca cu-si__
dos la - va. De - ja, de - ja, de - ja que llo - re, sus lá - gri - mas nos tra - e - rán__

__ cco-huacc - nin - chic - sa - ccey sa - ccey hi - na hua - cca chuh.__
__ la a - le gría De - ja, de - ja, de - ja que llo - re.__

They say that in Bethlehem the Child is crying.
Let him cry, he washes my sins away.
Let him, let him, let him cry
His tears will bring us happiness.
Let him, let him, let him cry.

Huaccacuspansi
Villancico de Ayachcho

Perú

Hua cca-cu-pan - si ma-ña-cun Hua-hua Hue cce-tas mu - nan Je sús hua cca-span Pi tacc mich-a -

cun ma-ña - cus ccan - ta Hua - hua tu - cu span cca par - cca-chap - tin?

//Con llanto está pidiendo ese Niño
lágrimas de amor quiere ese Niño//
Lágrimas de amor quiere ese Jesús
//¿Quién puede no garde tal pedido?//

With weeping the Child is pleading
tears of love the Child wants.
Jesus wants tears of love,
Who can deny him such a request?

This song should be realized without harmonic accompaniment. Simple percussion is effective.

Niño Diosmi paccarimum
villancico de Ayachcho

Perú

The Baby Jesus has been born in the stable of Bethlehem.
We all, kneeling, worship our God.
Sleep now, little Child and don't cry any more,
for our song and our harps will make you sleep.

This song of native origin, translated here into Spanish, is most fully realized without chordal accompaniment. A drone of an open fifth--F and C--can be played on each first beat in the first part. When the meter changes to 2/4, play a C octave on each first beat, returning to F-C on the last measure. This and the suggested drum accompaniment make an effective piece.

Vamos pastorcillos

Perú

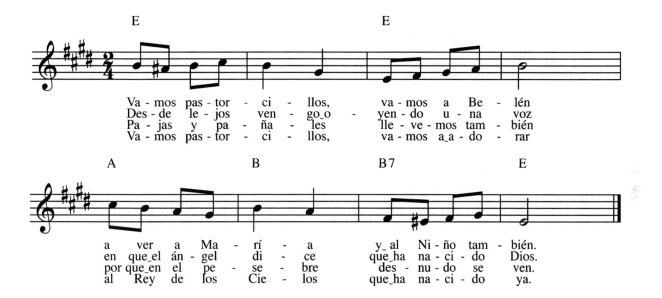

1. Let's go shepherds, let's go to Bethlehem
to see María and the Child also.

2. From afar I come hearing a voice
in which the angel says that God has been born.

3. Straw and diapers we bring also
because in the manger He is seen unclothed.

4. We are going, little shepherds, we are going to worship
the King of the Heavens who has now been born.

Los pastores de Belén

Uruguay

The shepherds of Bethlehem, all are going to look for wood
to warm the Baby who was born on Christmas Eve, shepherds arrive.
This is definitely a Good Night, the Good Night of Christmas.
The fish in the river leap and dance on seeing the birth of God.
The fish in the water leap and dance on seeing the birth of dawn.

Ya viene la vaca

Uruguay

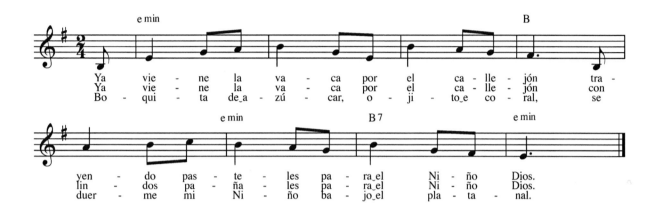

Ya vie - ne la va - ca por el ca - lle - jón tra -
Ya vie - ne la va - ca por el ca - lle - jón con
Bo - qui - ta de_a - zú - car, o - ji - to_e co - ral, se

yen - do pas - te - les pa - ra_el Ni - ño Dios.
lin - dos pa - ña - les pa - ra_el Ni - ño Dios.
duer - me mi Ni - ño ba - jo_el pla - ta - nal.

1. Here comes the cow through the alley carrying sweet foods for the Baby Jesus.

2. Here comes the cow through the alley with pretty diapers for the Baby Jesus.

3. Little mouth of sugar, little eye of jewel, my Baby sleeps under the banana trees.

The exact tune is sung in Argentina with the following words:
1. Ahí viene la vaca por el callejón trayendo la leche para el Niño Jesus.
   Here comes the cow through the alley carrying milk for the baby Jesus.
2. Ahí viene la vaca por el callejón juntando florcitas para el Niño Jesus.
   Here comes the cow through the alley gathering little flowers for the Baby Jesus.
3. Adios mi Niñito, boquita 'é coral, ojitos de estrellas que alumbran el mar.
   Goodbye my baby, little mouth of jewel, little eyes of stars that light up the sea.
4. Adios mi Niñito, p'al año 'hi volver trayendo en la mano un lindo clavel.
   Goodbye my baby, you'll return in a year carrying a lovely carnation in your hand.

Adorar al niño

Venezuela

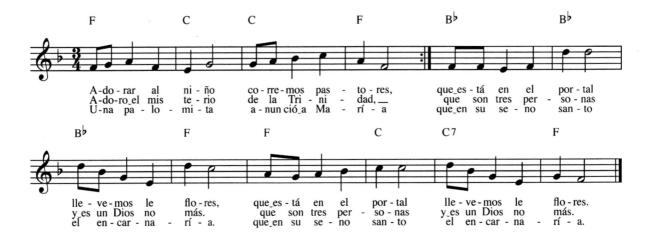

1. We shepherds hurry to worship the Child :‖
we bring flowers to him who is in the stable.:‖

2. I worship the mystery of the Trinity :‖
three persons and only one God.:‖

3. A little dove announced to María :‖
that in her holy womb would be the Incarnate One.:‖

Aguinaldo

Venezuela

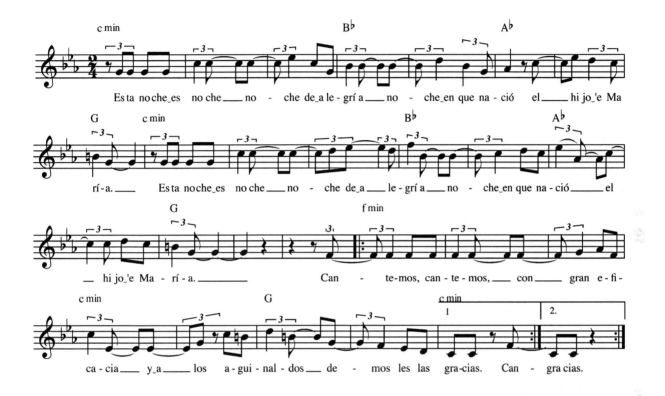

This night is a night of happiness, night when the son of María was born.
Let us sing with great enthusiasm the aguinaldos showing our thanks.

Niño lindo

Venezuela

Beautiful Child, I surrender myself before you, beautiful Child, you are my God :‖
Goodbye tender Infant, goodbye Child, goodbye,
Goodbye sweet beloved, goodbye sweet beloved, goodbye Child goodbye.

Villancico

Venezuela

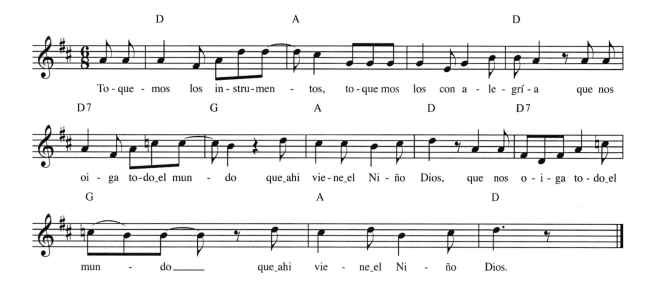

To - que - mos   los   in - stru - men - tos,   to - que mos   los   con a - le - grí - a   que nos

oi - ga to-do el mun - do   que ahi vie - ne el Ni - ño   Dios,   que nos o - i - ga to - do el

mun - do_____   que ahi vie - ne el Ni - ño   Dios.

We are playing the instruments, we are playing them with happiness,
let everyone hear us, for the Baby God comes.

Desde el Oriente han venido los tres Reyes al portal a solamente adorar al Niño que ha nacido.
   From the Orient have come the three Kings to the stable only to adore the Baby who is born.

Nació Jesús en Belén se bautizó en el Jordán, pereció en Jerusalén, visitó el seno de Abraham.
   Jesus was born in Bethlehem, baptized in the Jordan, appeared in Jerusalem, visited the bosom of
   Abraham.

Oh buen Dios de mis amores esta noche de contento presento a tu nacimiento un ramillete de flores.
   Oh God of my devotion this night of peace I present at your birthplace a cluster of flowers.

Central America

Costa Rica

Arrúarrú

Pastorcito miro

El Salvador
Guatemala
Honduras

See De todos partes

Nicaragua

Cascabel

Venid pastorcillos

Panamá

See De Todas Partes

Arrurrú

Costa Rica
arranged by Pilar Posada

Hush my child, for I have work to do, I have to wash the diapers and sit down to sew.
The Virgin washed them, San Jóse hung them out,
the child cried, I rocked him.
The roses and lilies are born,
the Child of God is born in Bethlehem. What a good thing!

Pastorcito, mira

Costa Rica

Little shepherd, look; little shepherd, come
to worship the Child who was born in Bethlehem.
A Child so beautiful, so lovely,
with such humility the King of the heavens who has been born!
His little eyes shine like the stars;
like a jasmine, and his little bare feet without socks.

Cascabel

as sung in Nicaragua

Cas ca bel, cas-ca bel, lin-do cas-ca bel, con sus no - tas de_a-le-grí-a va_a nun cian-do Él. __

Cas ca bel, cas-ca bel, lin-do cas-ca bel, con sus no-tas de_a-le-grí-a va_a-nun-cian-do Él. Ha lle

ga-do Na - vi - dad, En fa - mi -lia_a - le-gre_es-tá ce-le - bran-do No - che-bue - na en la

paz del san-to_ho-gar. Ha lle - ga-do Na - vi - dad. En fam - mi-lia_a - le-gre_es-tá ce-le-

brando Nochebuena en la paz del san to_ho gar. Cascabel, cascabel, lin do cas-ca bel, con sus no tas de_ale grí a

va_a nun cian do Él. __ Cas ca bel, cas ca bel, lin do cas-ca bel, con sus no-tas de_ale grí a va_a nun cian do Él.

Cascabel, cascabel, lovely cascabel, with your notes of happiness you are announcing Him.
Christmas has arrived, the happy family is celebrating Christmas Eve in the peace of the holy home.

Venid pastorcillos

Nicaragua

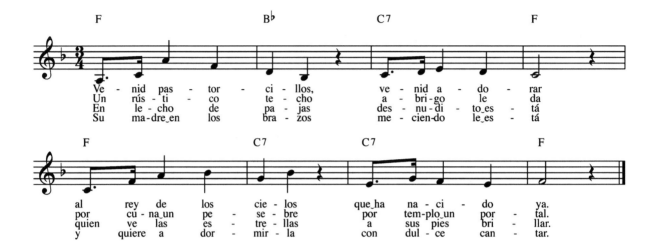

Ve - nid pas - tor - ci - llos, ve - nid a - do - rar
Un rús - ti - co te - cho a - bri-go le da
En le - cho de pa - jas des - nu-di - to_es - tá
Su ma-dre_en los bra - zos me - cien-do le_es - tá

al rey de los cie - los que_ha na - ci - do ya.
por cu - na_un pe - se - bre por tem-plo_un por - tal.
quien ve las es - tre - llas a sus pies bri - llar.
y quiere a dor - mir - la con dul - ce can - tar.

1. Come shepherds, come to worship the King of the heavens who has just been born.

2. A rustic roof gives him shelter, for a cradle a manger, for his temple a stable.

3. He lies naked in a bed of straw, he sees the stars shining at his feet.

4. His mother rocks him in her arms and lulls him to sleep with sweet singing.

De Todas Partes

A Belén
¡Ay! del chiquirritín
Campana sobre campana
Esa noche yo baila
La Marimorena
Los peces en el río
Rin, rin
Riu, riu, chiu
Ya viene la vieja

A Belén

I have to go to Bethlehem, come with me, little shepherd friend.
The Child has been born, chirulí.
I have bought a beautiful flute, chirulí,
for the Child, chiquitín, chirulí, chirulí, we are going without delay.

I have bought a beautiful drum, rataplán,
for the Child, rataplán, rataplán, we are going without delay.

¡Ay! del chiquirritín

¡Ay! del chi-qui-rri - tín, chi qui rri qui - tín, me-ti - di-to en tre pa - jas. ¡Ay! del chi-qui-rri - tín, chi qui rri qui - tín, que ri - do, que ri - di-to del al - ma. En-tre un buey y u-na mu - la, Dios ha na - ci - do y en un po-bre pe - se - bre le ha re - co-gi - do. Por de - ba jo del ar - co del por-ta-li - co, se des-cu-bre a Ma - rí - a, Jo sé, y el Ni - ño.

Ay del chiquirritín, chiquirriquitín, lying in the straw.
Ay del chiquirritín, chiquirriquitín, beloved of my soul.
Between an ox and a mule God has been born
and in a poor stable he has been placed.
Beneath the archway of the little stable
María, San José, and the Child are discovered.

Campana sobre campana

Mexico

Bell after bell after bell. Come to the window to see the Baby in the cradle.
Bells of Bethlehem the angels sing. What news do they bring me?
Where are you going, little shepherd now that you've gathered your flock?
I am taking cheese, butter, and wine to the stable.

Esa noche yo baila

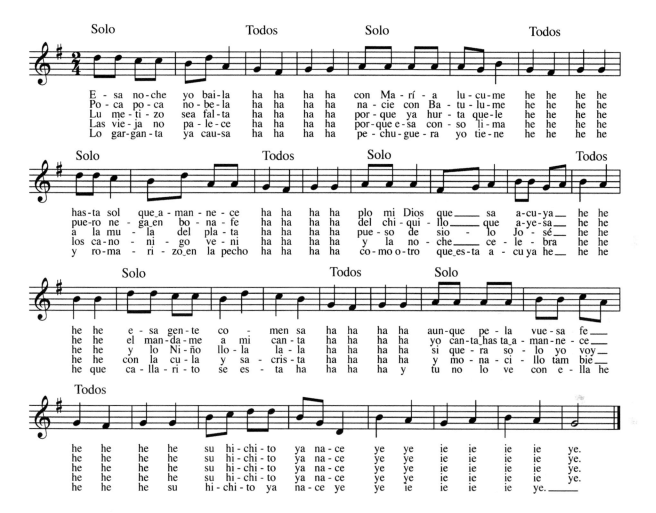

The mood of this villancico is one of great festivity--to dance until dawn, for the Baby is born.
It is an example of *villancico de negros*, reflecting the dances of the African slaves and domestic
servants during the period of Spanish colonialism. It is to be found in the musical archive of the
Santa Clara monastery in Cochabamba, Bolivia. Although only the melody and words were found,
a writer at the end of the eighteenth century suggested that accompanying instruments might have
been an earthenware jar (*botija*) played with the hands rather than mallets, small nose flutes, and
jawbone (*quixada*) of a horse or donkey skinned and dried, rubbed with a smooth stick. The language
is archaic.

La Marimorena

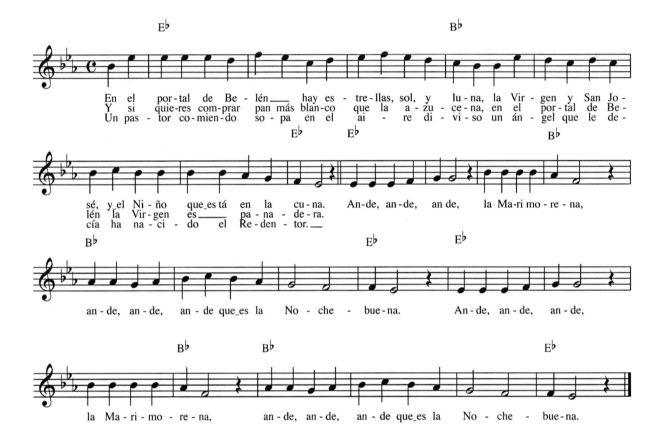

1. In a stall in Bethlehem there are stars, the sun and moon,
the Virgin and San José, and the Baby in the cradle.

   Move along, Marimorena,
   Move along, for it is Christmas Eve.

2. And if you want to buy bread whiter than the lily,
in the stall of Bethlehem the Virgin is the baker.

3. A shepherd eating soup in the open air
saw an angel who told him the Redeemer had been born.

Los peces en el río

The Virgin is combing her hair, between the curtains,
her hair is golden, her combs of fine silver.
See how the fish drink, the fish in the river,
See how they drink on seeing the newborn God,
they drink and drink and they drink again on seeing the newborn God.

Rin rin

1. A burro is going toward Bethlehem, rin rin
yo me la remendaba, yo me la remendé, yo me eché un remiendo, yo me lo quité
laden with chocolate, she carries her chocolate pot, rin rin
yo me la remendaba, yo me la remendé, yo me eché un remiendo, yo me lo quité
her grinder, and her oven.
María, María, come quickly
for they are eating the little chocolates.

This song and ¡Ay! del chiquirritin come obviously come from the same roots, but both the tune and the words are different.

Riu, riu, chiu

Mateo Flecha the elder
1481-1553

Ri u, ri u, chi us, la guar da ri be ra; Dios guar da el lo bo de nues tra cor

de ra; Dios guar da el lo bo de nues tra cor de ra.

Riu, riu, chiu, the riverbank protects it;
God protects our lamb from the wolf.

This sixteenth century villancico could have come with the first Spanish explorers to the New World
where it is still sung. The language--archaic to us in modern times--is that of the time it was written.
It has many verses, two of which are included here. Each is followed by the estribillo written above.

El lobo rabioso la quiso morder;
bas Dios poderoso la supo defendeer.
Cristo patriarca de carne vestido;
ni pudiese pecar, ni-aun original esta Virgen

    The rabid wolf wanted to bite her;
    but the powerful God knew how to defend her.
    Christ incarnate;
    this Virgin was even without original sin.

Yo vi mil garzones que andavan cantando,
por aqui bolando, haciendo mil sones,
diziendo a gascones "Gloria sea en el cielo,
y paz en el suelo que es Jesús nascieta."

I saw a thousand herons singing as they went
flying by, making thousands of sounds,
saying "Glory be in heaven
and peace on earth for Jesus is born."

    translated by Bruce Cockburn

Ya viene la vieja

1. Here comes the old woman with the *aguinaldo*,
it appears too much, she's taking some away from it.
Green vines, leaves of the lemon tree,
the Virgin María, Mother of the Lord.

2. Here come the Kings through the sandy lands,
they're taking many precious diapers to the Child.

3. Melchior brings gold, Gaspar incense,
and Balthasar brings fragrant myrrh.

The Recipes

Few things are more deeply entrenched in memory and in reality than the foods we are accustomed to have at Christmas time. The recipes here, gathered from personal information, from friends, and from the internet, are representative of the twenty areas of Spanish-speaking peoples we cover in North, Central, and South America.

Many of the recipes have been tried out in my kitchen and in the kitchens of friends and family. Some seem strange in their combination of ingredients—such as rice with coca cola. Some had ingredients so difficult to find that substitutions are suggested—such as corn husks or even foil for banana leaves, or bananas for plantains. And the titles of some give cause for a double take, such as *Niños envueltos* (wrapped-up children) or *Pavo con moros* (turkey stuffed with Moors).

This is by no definition a comprehensive recipe book, but it is a fair sampling of holiday foods in the various countries. It is arranged with recipes by country rather than in categorical or alphabetical order.

One food is so widely used as a Christmas centerpiece, *lechón asado* (roast pork), that it isn't reasonable to assign it to any one or two countries, but it must be included in any listing of Christmas recipes, like the carols grouped under *De Todos Partes*.

Lechón asado

The best way, the most traditional way, is to roast an entire pig over an open fire. This calls for an all-day affair—the day before it is to be eaten—with family and friends gathered to help. Often the women will be in the house preparing other foods for the Christmas table while the men are outside with the slowly cooking pork, watching and turning it until the outside is very crisp. If, however, such a ceremony cannot easily be handled, you can substitute with a smaller piece of meat and your kitchen oven with this recipe.

> 6 pounds of pork, thigh or shoulder is best
> 5 teaspoons salt
> 5 garlic cloves
> 1 teaspoon pepper
> 1/2 teaspoon oregano
> 3 tablespoons vegetable oil
> 1 tablespoon vinegar

Wash the meat and make several incisions in it. Put salt in the incisions. Mix together garlic, pepper, oregano, and 1 tablespoon salt and rub it over the pork. Mix the vinegar and oil and spread over the spices. Cover and refrigerate for 1 day. On the next day remove the meat 2 hours before putting it in the oven. Preheat the oven to 350 degrees. Cook the pork for 3 and a half hours, then raise the temperature to 375 degrees and cook another hour.

The Caribbean Islands

Cuba

Cristianos y Moros

> 1 pound dry black beans (soak overnight, drain before cooking)
> 1 tablespoon vegetable oil
> 4 cloves garlic minced
> 1 tablespoon olive oil
> 1 teaspoon salt
> 1 bell pepper chopped
> 1/4 teaspoon oregano
> 1/4 teaspoon cumin
> 1/4 teaspoon pepper
> 1 pound long grain rice
> 1 large onion chopped

Bring beans to boiling in 6 cups of water. Remove from heat and let stand about an hour. Continue cooking until beans are done, 2 to 3 hours. Place the vegetable oil and rice in a pot and stir until the grains of rice are oily. Add garlic, onion, bell pepper, spices, and salt. Add 2 cups liquid from the beans, bring to boiling, then lower heat, cover the pot and cook about 20 minutes, until liquid is absorbed and rice is tender. Drain beans and combine with rice mixture.

Cuba

Buñuelos

3 tablespoons butter
3/4 cup sugar
3 eggs well beaten
grated rind of 1 lemon
1 cup water
flour
oil for cooking

Cream butter and sugar, add lemon rind. Add beaten eggs, water, and enough flour to make a soft dough. Roll out on board and cut off small pieces. Drop into deep fat which must be not too hot. When brown, remove and drain. Sprinkle with powdered sugar and cinnamon or with honey.

Dominican Republic

Gingebre

> 8 cinnamon sticks
> 5 cups boiling water
> 2/3 ounce fresh ginger peeled and diced
> sugar to taste

Pour boiling water over cinnamon sticks. Simmer for about 10 minutes. Add ginger and simmer 5 minutes more. Strain and add sugar to taste.

> This is different—with the sharp, spicy taste of the cinnamon and ginger.
> It's a good winter drink and could use a shot of rum for a hot rum toddy.

Dominican Republic

Pastelitos

> 4 cups flour
> 1/2 teaspoon salt
> 1/2 cup butter
> 2 eggs
> 1 egg yolk
> 1 cup cold water
> 3 cups prepared beef hash, cooked chicken, or cheese
> oil for frying

Combine flour and salt. Cut butter into dry ingredients. Mix water, eggs, and egg yolk and gradually stir into flour mixture. Knead until the dough is smooth. Let dough stand half an hour at room temperature. Roll out to about 1/4 inch thickness. Cut into 3-inch circles. Place 1 tablespoon of filling in the center of half the pastry rounds. Moisten the edges with water and place another round on top of the filling. Seal the edges tightly. Fry in 1 inch of medium hot oil until golden brown. Remove and drain. To avoid frying, I brushed the pastelitos with olive oil and baked at 350 degrees for about 15 minutes. Pretty good.

Puerto Rico

Pavo con Moros

Marinade for turkey:
8 garlic cloves mashed with 1 teaspoon salt
1 tablespoon cumin
1/2 teaspoon pepper
1 teaspoon oregano
1/3 cup orange juice
1/3 cup olive oil
1 large onion chopped

Mix all ingredients together, rub a turkey inside and out, and place it in a roasting pan. Cover and leave overnight in the refrigerator.

Moros:
1 1/2 cups black beans
1/4 cup olive oil
6 strips bacon chopped
2 1/2 cups white onion chopped
2 1/2 cups bell pepper diced
4 garlic cloves crushed
1 tablespoon cumin
1 teaspoon oregano
1 bay leaf
3 tablespoons white vinegar
2 tablespoons tomato paste
2 teaspoons pepper
4 1/3 cups chicken stock
3 cups long grain white rice

(continued)

Pavo con moros (continued)

Cover the beans with about 4 cups of water. Boil for 3 minutes. Remove from heat and let stand, covered, for an hour. Drain and rinse the beans. Add enough water to cover, bring to a boil, then reduce heat, cover, and cook until tender, about an hour. Drain.

Rinse the rice with cold water. In a large 8-quart pan, sauté the bacon, onion, and bell pepper in olive oil. Add garlic and sauté another minute or two. Add tomato paste, beans, oregano, cumin, bay leaf, and vinegar. Cook about 5 minutes, stirring gently. Add chicken stock and rinsed rice. Bring to a boil, then reduce heat, cover, and cook until rice is done, about 20 minutes. Add salt and pepper to taste, remove bay leaf.

1/2 pound thick-sliced bacon
1/2 cup white wine

Stuff the turkey with the moros. Cover with bacon slices and pour wine over the top. Roast at 325 degrees until fully cooked, allowing about 25 minutes per pound. Cover with foil if turkey begins to brown too quickly.

You could use a large turkey breast or other parts of a turkey rather than the whole bird, with perhaps half or a third the recipe for the stuffing. The effect and taste are not quite the same, but it is a good substitute if you're not up to dealing with the whole turkey. Place the stuffing in a baking pan; lay the turkey pieces on it, cover with bacon and wine.

Puerto Rico

Coquito

2 15-ounce cans coconut cream
1 can condensed milk
1 can evaporated milk
4 egg yolks beaten
1/2 cup cognac
1 teaspoon vanilla
1 quart white rum
1 tablespoon cinnamon

Blend egg yolks and condensed milk gradually. Add and blend all other ingredients. Refrigerate. Serve cold.

South America

Argentina

Alfajores

Cookies:
1 1/2 cups unsalted butter
1 cup powdered sugar
2 tablespoons granulated sugar
1/4 teaspoon salt
1/4 teaspoon almond extract
1/2 teaspoon vanilla extract
1/3 cup ground almonds
3 cups unbleached all-purpose flour

Cream butter and powdered sugar until fluffy. Stir in salt, extracts, almonds, and flour. Mix well. Wrap and chill 30 minutes. Roll out chilled dough to 1/4 inch thickness. Cut in 2 1/2 inch circles. Bake at 350 degrees for 12-14 minutes. Cool.

Filling:
2 cups packed brown sugar
1 cup half and half
3 tablespoons unsalted butter
1/2 teaspoon vanilla extract

Heat brown sugar and half and half over medium heat. While this is cooking, brush the inner sides of the pan with a pastry brush dipped in cold water to wipe away grainy sugar crystals. Heat until mixture reaches

(continued)

Alfajores (continued)

soft ball stage, about 240 degrees. Remove from heat, cool to about 110 degrees. Stir in butter and beat until mixture is thickened. Add vanilla. (If mixture is too thin, add powdered sugar; if too thick, beat longer or add additional half and half.)

Spread some filling on a cooled cookie. Top with another cookie and press together. Dust tops with powdered sugar. A recipe from Uruguay, *Dulce de Leche,* Can also be used as a filling for *alfajores.*

Argentina

Niños Envueltos

2 medium cabbages
2 cups rice
1 cup chicken ground or cut in small cubes
2 tomatoes chopped
4 tablespoons parsley chopped
3 cloves garlic chopped
2 teaspoons pimiento chopped
1/2 cup oil
1 tablespoon butter melted
2 cubes chicken bouillon
salt to taste

Soak the cabbages in hot water to loosen and separate the leaves. Mix very well the rice and other ingredients except bouillon cubes. Place 2 or 3 tablespoons of the rice mixture in each cabbage leaf. Roll each cabbage leaf, pressing the ends together. Place the *niños* carefully side by side in the bottom of a large pot. Add second and third layers. Add the bouillon cubes dissolved in 5 cups of water. Bring to a boil, then cook over low heat 25 to 30 minutes, until the rice is done. (NOTE: The *niños* can be prepared a day early, refrigerated, then cooked the next day.)

This is an interesting variation of a cabbage roll. Jane had a hard time with the cabbage leaves, and she finally made them more like cabbage sandwiches, placing the filling between two leaves, then tying the leaves together. Flavorful, tasty.

Bolivia

Coconut Muffins

> 2 tablespoons soft butter
> scant 1/2 cup sugar
> 1 tablespoon orange extract
> 1/4 teaspoon cloves
> 1/4 teaspoon cinnamon
> 4 egg yolks
> 1 egg white
> 1 cup flour
> 1 teaspoon baking powder
> 1 cup grated coconut
> 1 1/2 tablespoons melted butter

Pre-heat oven to 350 degrees. Mix butter, sugar, extract, and spices together until sugar starts to dissolve. Mix in egg yolks. Beat egg white until stiff, then fold into mixture. Combine
flour and baking powder and add gradually into mixture. Add coconut. Grease individual muffin tins or paper muffin holders with melted butter; fill each until about 3/4 full. Bake 12 to 15 minutes until muffins have risen and become light brown on top.

> Sweet and savory muffins with an interesting mixture of
> spices. Mary Helen warns that the dough will be stiff if dry
> grated coconut is used, and she suggests adding a half cup of
> milk. If, instead, you make them with fresh grated coconut,
> the dough will be much more pliable.

Bolivia

Picana de Pollo

1 chicken cut into 8 pieces (or chicken breasts)
2 cups white wine
1/2 cup green peas
1 bay leaf
1 sliced onion
1 cup peeled and chopped tomato
3 carrots cut into strips
1 green chile cut into 8 pieces
1 small branch thyme minced
1 celery rib chopped
1/4 cup parsley
freshly ground pepper
2 cups broth (or water)
16 round slices corn on the cob
1/2 cup raisins
8 whole potatoes

Place all ingredient except potatoes in large casserole. Mix well, then add potatoes on top of other ingredients. Cook over low heat for about two hours. To serve, place a piece of chicken, a potato, and 2 corn slices in deep individual serving dishes; add broth and vegetable mixture.

Jane used sugar snap peas, her choice of wine was Chablis, and she used chicken breasts rather than the whole chicken. Before serving she cut the meat off the bones, cut it into "reasonable" size pieces and threw away the skin. She took it to a church supper where it achieved stellar success!

Chile

Pollo al Pil Pil

1 roasted chicken
3/4 pound prawns
2 green chiles diced
2 onions sliced
4 large cooked potatoes diced
olive oil to sauté chiles and onions
salt and oregano to taste
1 1/2 cups chicken broth

Saute chiles and onions with oregano in olive oil. When they are tender, add prawns and cook over slow heat for about 10 minutes. Place the chicken in a baking pan, add broth and about 2/3 of the prawn mixture. Bake at 350 degrees until the chicken is thoroughly heated. Add potatoes and the rest of the prawn mixture. Heat until warmed throughout.

If you purchase an already roasted chicken, you have the basis for a fast and easy way to create a delicious dinner!

Chile

Pastel de Chocolo

cut kernels from 6 large ears of corn grated
8 leaves of fresh basil chopped
1 teaspoon salt
3 tablespoons butter
1/2 cup milk
4 onions chopped
3 tablespoons oil
1 pound ground beef
1 teaspoon cumin
4 hard-boiled eggs sliced
1 cup black olives
1 cup raisins
12 pieces chicken
2 tablespoons powdered sugar

Brown chicken in hot oil and set aside. Heat corn and basil in butter. Add milk gradually, stirring until it thickens. Cook over low heat for 5 minutes. Set aside. Fry onions in oil until transparent, add ground beef and stir to brown. Season with salt, pepper, and cumin. Spread the meat/onion mixture in a baking pan. Arrange hard-boiled egg slices, olives, and raisins over this mixture. Place chicken pieces over this and cover with corn mixture. Sprinkle powdered sugar over the top. Bake at 400 degrees for 30-35 minutes until the crust is golden brown. Serve hot.

There was no cumin in the cupboard, but there was cilantro so I used it—but only 1/2 teaspoon. No fresh basil, but 1 tablespoon of ground basil seemed about right. A can of corn took the place of fresh grated kernels but did not produce the thick crust grated corn would have. Since this was to be supper for just my husband and me, I divided the recipe, using approximately a third of the measurements here.

Colombia

Hojuelas

1/2 cup butter
3 cups flour
1 tablespoon sugar
5 tablespoons orange juice
3 tablespoons ice cold water
cooking oil

Mix butter and flour with two forks. Add salt, sugar, juice, and water. Blend. Roll out dough and fold it in half. Repeat this two more times, then chill in refrigerator. When chilled, roll out very thin and cut into diagonal strips. Make a slit in the center of each strip. Deep fry in cooking oil until golden. Drain on paper towels and sprinkle with sugar.

These were very good—crispy and hot. I had to add a little more water than the recipe calls for.

Colombia

Natilla

      1 quart milk
      1 cup cornstarch
      1/2 cup sugar
      2 cinnamon sticks or ground cinnamon to taste
      1 cup shredded coconut

Dissolve cornstarch in the milk. Add sugar. Cook over low heat, stirring constantly. When the sugar is completely dissolved and the mixture begins to thicken, add the cinnamon and coconut. When it is very thick, pour into a large serving dish. Serve either hot or cold.

This is the traditional Colombian Christmas pudding prepared outside in an enormous *olla,* with all the family taking turns at stirring.

Colombia

Chicken Soup

4 chicken breasts
1 yam cut into 8 pieces
2 onions cut into quarters
1 green bell pepper
1 handful of green beans, cut into 1inch pieces
2 ears of corn cut into quarters
2 ribs of celery cut into 1inch pieces
2 large carrots cut into 1inch pieces
2 pounds potatoes, peeled and cubed
6 cloves garlic
2 chicken bouillon cubes
1 tablespoon salt
1/2 teaspoon pepper

Put the chicken in a large pot and add 8 cups of water. Bring to a boil, then reduce heat to simmer. Simmer for 10 minutes, skimming the foam from the surface from time to time. Add vegetables, garlic, bouillon cubes, salt, and pepper. Return to boil, then reduce to simmer. Partially cover the pot and continue on simmer for 1 1/2 hours. Remove chicken. Break up potatoes slightly to thicken soup. Pull the meat from the chicken bones and add to soup when it is ready to serve.

(continued)

Chicken Soup (continued)

Aji:

> 4 green onions
> 1 tomato peeled and seeded
> 1 small onion
> 2 chiles stems and seeds removed
> 3 tablespoons vinegar
> 1/4 teaspoon salt

Pulse ingredients in blender or food processor until they are finely minced.

Place garnishes—aji, sour cream, avocados—in separate bowls for diners to add to their soup servings as they choose.

Ecuador

Rompope

      1 quart milk
      1 pound sugar
      2 cinnamon sticks
      1 bottle rum or other liquor
      8 egg yolks

    Boil the milk, sugar, and cinnamon sticks together until the mixture turns pink. Remove from heat and cool. Beat the egg yolks. When the milk mixture is cool, add the egg yolks, then boil again for 5 minutes. Remove from heat, cool. Add liquor. Chill.

    This is very good. I made the recipe using just 1/4 of each ingredient, just right for a bit of nog for two people. Be sure to cool the milk before adding the egg yolks or the mixture will curdle.

Ecuador

Arroz con Coca Cola y Pasas

3 cups rice
3 1/2 cups coca cola
1 teaspoon salt
1 tablespoon oil
1 cup raisins
1 onion chopped
1 bell pepper chopped
butter
cream
nuts
cubed ham (optional)

Sauté onion and bell pepper in a spoonful of butter. Add rice, coca cola, salt, and oil. Bring to a boil, then cover and simmer until rice is done, about 20 minutes. Add raisins, nuts and (optional) ham. Serve in individual dishes with a dollop of cream on each serving.

Paraguay

Sopa Paraguaysa

8 tablespoons butter
1 large onion chopped
1 cup cottage cheese
1 cup grated Muenster or Cheddar cheese
2 cups cornmeal
2 cups fresh corn kernels or 1 can creamed corn
1 teaspoon salt
1 cup milk
6 eggs separated

Heat half the butter to cook the onion until tender. In a separate container combine the other half of the butter with the cottage cheese and mix thoroughly. Add the grated cheese, onion, cornmeal, corn, salt, milk, and egg yolks. Mix thoroughly. Beat the egg whites until stiff, then fold into the batter. Pour into a greased and floured 10 x 13 inch baking pan. Bake in preheated oven at 400 degrees for about 50 minutes, until a toothpick inserted in the middle comes out clean.

This is a spoon bread, similar to cornbread. Very good. Adding chopped green chiles would be nice also.

Paraguay

Pollo de Navidad

> 1 large chicken
> 1/4 cup butter
> 1/4 bottle red wine
> 1/4 bottle white wine
> 1/4 bottle sherry
> juice of 1 lemon
> 2 cloves garlic crushed
> 1 onion minced
> salt to taste
>
> Stuffing:
> 1/4 pound ground beef
> 1/4 pound ground pork
> 1/2 cup almonds
> green apple diced
> 1/2 cup raisins
> 4 slices bacon diced

Marinate the chicken in the wines while preparing the stuffing. Sauté the meats, apple, raisins, almonds, and bacon in a little butter. Mix garlic and onion and add lemon juice. Mis all ingredients together. Rub the chicken inside and out with softened buter. Stuff chicken, cover with aluminum foil, and cook at 400 degrees about 40 minutes.

Perú

Pavo de Navidad

> 10-12 pound turkey
> 2 cups pecans or other nuts chopped
> 2 onions finely diced
> 1/2 cup celery chopped
> 8 cups day-old bread cubed
> 2 teaspoons salt
> 1 teaspoon dill weed
> 1/2 cup butter
> 1/2 cup boiling water

Mix nuts with onion, celery, and bread. Add salt and dill weed. Melt butter in boiling water and add to bread mixture. Mix well; stuff cavities of the turkey, and close them securely. Bake at 350 degrees, about 25 minutes per pound.

> I tried this stuffing with a large turkey breast, cut down the salt by half, and increased the water to 1 cup. Place the stuffing on the bottom of the pan and lay the turkey breast on top. Cover and bake at 350 degrees 2 1/2 – 3 hours, depending on size of the turkey breast.

Perú

Clerico

wine, red or sweet white
mineral water
apples peeled and cubed
oranges separated into segments
dark and light grapes
cubed melon
cubed pineapple
sugar

Wash and cut the fruit. Cover it with sugar and leave it to marinate in the refrigerator for 12 hours. Add wine and mineral water and chill thoroughly.

Uruguay

Dulce de Leche

> 4 quarts milk
> 2 cups sugar
> 1 teaspoon baking soda
> few drops of vanilla

Scald the milk in a large pan. Add sugar and soda and cook over low heat until it thickens and becomes caramel color. Stir often with a wooden spoon. Cooking time will be about an hour. When done, add vanilla. When cool and thickened, spread between alfajores or serve as caramel pudding.

Jane said she had fun making this recipe. She served it as a pudding which had the consistency of sweetened condensed milk. (The recipe for alfajores is in the Argentina section.)

Uruguay

Panettone

> 2 tablespoons dry yeast
> 1 cup warm water
> 4 tablespoons butter
> 1/2 cup sugar
> 1 teaspoon salt
> 2 tablespoons grated lemon rind
> 2 tablespoons orange juice
> 3 eggs
> 4 1/2 to 5 1/2 cups flour
> 1 cup chopped dried glazed fruit (optional: soak in cognac)
> chopped nuts (optional)
> 1 egg plus 1 tablespoon water for painting

Mix yeast and warm water; let it rest 5 minutes, then stir till dissolved. Cream butter and sugar. Add and mix well salt, lemon rind, orange juice, eggs, and yeast. Add flour gradually to make a soft dough. Add glazed fruit and nuts. Continue adding flour until dough is easy to work with. Form into 1 large or 2 small round loaves. Cover and let rise until nearly double, 2 to 3 hours. Punch down and re-form into loaves. Place on greased baking sheet. Cover and let rise again until nearly double, about 1 hour. Paint the surface with beaten egg and water. Bake at 350 degrees 35-40 minutes. If browning too quickly, cover loosely with foil.

Mary Helen soaked dried fruit in Grand Marnier and used fresh orange juice. She said she used a beater for the dough until she'd added about 4 cups of flour. After that she

(continued)

Panettone (continued)

kneaded it by hand as she added the nuts and enough more flour until it was not too sticky to work with. She liked this recipe because it reminded her of the panettone she had known in Italy.

Venezuela

Pan de Jamón

> 1 1/2 cups water
> 5 teaspoons granulated yeast
> 1 teaspoon sugar
>
> Dough:
> 1 3/4 cups butter
> 1 quart warm milk
> 8 cups flour
> 1 teaspoon salt
> 1 teaspoon sugar
>
> Filling:
> 1 1/2 pounds thinly sliced ham
> 1/2 pound bacon, cooked, crumbled
> 1 3/4 cups butter
> 2 cups olives
> 2 cups raisins
> 1 egg beaten

Mix water and sugar with yeast and let stand 15 minutes. Add butter, sugar, and salt to warm milk. Pour milk onto flour, mix, add yeast. Mix well and knead until smooth, about 15 minutes. Place in oiled bowl, cover with a damp cloth, and let rise an hour. When double in size, roll out dough, coat with butter, and place ham on it. Cover with bacon, olives, and raisins. Roll like a jelly roll and brush edge to seal it. Bake at 350 degrees about 45 minutes.

Venezuela

Hallaca

First filling:
1 pound top round cut into 1/2 inch cubes
1 pound pork cut into 1/2 inch cubes
1/4 pound bacon cut into 1/2 inch pieces
3 tomatoes peeled and seeded
1 onion chopped
3 cloves garlic
1 tablespoon salt
2 teaspoons marjoram
1/4 cup capers
1 onion diced
1 tablespoon mustard
1/4 cup wine vinegar
1 bell pepper cut in 1/2 inch pieces
1 teaspoon Worcestershire sauce
salt and pepper to taste
1/2 cup raisins

Place meats in a large pan. Puree tomatoes with onion and garlic. Add salt, marjoram, and onion. Combine with meats, cover, and bring to a boil. Lower heat and continue cooking until meats are tender, about 2 hours. When meats are tender, add capers, pickles, vinegar, bell pepper, Worcestershire sauce, sugar, salt and pepper. Over high heat cook the filling, stirring, until almost all the liquid has evaporated, about 10 minutes. Add raisins and set aside. (This filling can be made a day ahead.)

Masa dough:
2/3 cup lard
1 teaspoon annatto seeds (optional)
2 cups masa harina

(continued)

Hallaca (continued)

        1 teaspoon salt
        1 teaspoon cayenne pepper
        1 2/3 cups warm water

    Melt 1/3 cup lard over low heat with annatto seeds. Simmer 2 or 3 minutes. Whip remaining lard until fluffy. Beat in masa harina, salt, cayenne pepper, and water. Finally beat in melted, strained lard, discarding annatto seeds. Form dough into 24 balls.

        Second filling:
        1 pound cooked, shredded chicken
        4 hard-boiled eggs sliced
        1/4 cup almonds
        2 ounces pimientos sliced
        5 ounces stuffed olives sliced
        Tabasco sauce to taste

Soak 24 corn husks in hot water until they are pliable.

    Mix chicken, almonds, pimientos, and olives together. Place a ball of masa dough in the center of 12 corn husks. Flatten dough to 1/8-inch thickness. Top each masa-coated husk with a small amount of each of the two fillings after they have cooled. Distribute hard-boiled egg slices. Sprinkle on Tabasco sauce to taste. Place each filled hallaca on a second corn husk to guard against leaking. Roll each husk tightly, folding in the ends or tying with twine. Steam in large pot for about an hour. Serve very hot.

        Hallaca is the hallmark Christmas dish of Venezuela, labor-intensive though they may be. Of course they are best wrapped in banana leaves. Second-best are corn husks, and if all else fails, they can be wrapped in foil.

Central America

Costa Rica

Brandied Eggnog

    5 scoops vanilla ice cream
    1/4 cup brandy
    1/4 cup milk
    2 tablespoons Grand Marnier liqueur
    1/4 teaspoon nutmeg

Combine all ingredients in blender and blend until smooth and frothy. Pour into four glasses and sprinkle with additional nutmeg.

Costa Rica

Pupusas Revueltas

Masa:
3 cups masa meal
2 cups water

Mix to consistency of cookie dough and shape into thin patties about 3 inches in diameter, 1/8-inch thick. Cover with damp cloth.

Filling:
Monterey Jack cheese grated
1/4 pound red beans
1 minced onion
1 clove garlic
1/4 teaspoon salt
1/2 tablespoon olive oil

Cook beans with onion and garlic. When done, place them in a blender with salt and 1/4 cup cooking liquid from the beans. Blend into puree, then cook in olive oil for about 15 minutes.

Assembly:

Place half a tablespoon each of bean mixture and cheese on top of a patty. Cover with second patty. Press edges together to seal. Cook on non-stick griddle until brown, about 4 minutes per side.

El Salvador

Arroz Verde

2 tablespoons butter
1 pound rice
1 clove garlic minced
1 small onion chopped
10 green chiles without seeds
3 cups water
1 teapsoon salt
1/2 cup garbanzos
4 ounces grated cheese
1/2 cup cream

Brown garlic and onion in butter. Add rice and cook for 2 minutes. Liquefy in a blender the green chiles, water, and salt. Add to rice mixture and bring to boil, then lower heat, add garbanzos, and cook 40 minutes. When done, let it rest for about 10 minutes. In a greased baking dish place a layer of the rice/garbanzo mixture, then a layer of cheese and cream. Repeat for 2 more layers. Bake at 350 degrees for 30 minutes.

That's a lot of chile. You might want to use fewer than 10. I used 6, and they made it plenty *picante*.

El Salvador

Pupusas

> 4 cups flour
> 2 teaspoons salt
> 2 teaspoons baking powder
> 4 tablespoons shortening (not liquid oil)
> 1 1/2 cups warm water
> 1/2 pound shredded Muenster cheese

Cut shortening into combined dry ingredients. Add warm water gradually and work dough with hands until manageable. Knead 15 to 20 times, then allow to stand for 10 minutes. Form dough into balls the size of an egg. Roll each out into tortillas 6 inches in diameter, or flatten them with your hands. Sprinkle cheese on half the tortillas, then cover with the other half of the tortillas. Seal. Place one *pupusa* at a time on a hot ungreased skillet. Cook 2 minutes on each side. Serve topped with shredded cabbage and carrots.

These are also good stuffed with refried beans.

Guatemala

Flan

    1 cup sugar, divided
    3 1/2 cups milk
    6 eggs
    2 egg yolks
    1 teaspoon vanilla
    1/4 teaspoon almond flavoring
    1/3 cup chopped almonds

Heat half a cup of sugar in a heavy pan. Stir constantly until it melts and turns light brown. Immediately pour it into a 1 1/2 quart oven-proof dish and tilt to coat all the sides. In another pan scald the milk. Beat eggs and yolks until light, then beat in remaining half cup of sugar. Stir in the scalded milk, vanilla, and almond flavoring. Pour into the mold and place in a pan of boiling water. Bake at 350 degrees for 50 minutes or until set. Let cool, then chill. Loosen the edges and unmold on a platter. Sprinkle with chopped almonds.

Mary Helen's notes: This made a sweet, soft, golden custard with a good texture. The quantity of almonds seemed too much; perhaps 1/4 cup would be enough. The almonds softened a bit on the second day, and I liked this better.

Guatemala

Buñuelos

> 1 cup water
> 1/2 teaspoon anise seed
> 1/4 teaspoon salt
> 1/8 teaspoon soda
> 1 1/4 cups sifted flour
> 5 eggs
> oil for frying

Mix water, anise seed, and salt. Bring to a boil, then add soda and flour. Remove pan from heat and beat until flour is well mixed. Let the dough cool. Add eggs one at a time, completely mixing in each one before adding the next. Let the dough sit for at least an hour, covered with plastic or cloth. Form into 15 to 20 small balls. Drop into hot oil and fry until golden brown. Drain on paper towels.

> Glaze:
> 1/2 –3/4 cup sugar
> 1 cup water
> 1 cinnamon stick

Mix ingredients and bring to a boil. Lower heat and simmer about 5 minutes. Cool slightly and add 1 teaspooon vanilla. Cover *buñuelos* with glaze.

Honduras

Torrejas

3 cups brown sugar
3 cinnamon sticks
3 cups water
4 eggs
French bread

Boil brown sugar and cinnamon sticks in water for 10 minutes. Beat eggs and slice bread. Dip each slice into beaten eggs. Fry in hot fat until well browned. Place in baking pan and cover with cinnamon/sugar sauce. Bake at 250 degrees for 20 minutes. Serve warm.

Honduras

Enchiladas Catrachas

8 corn tortillas
1 pound lean ground beef
1/4-1/2 pound grated cheese
5 cloves garlic
1 onion
1 bell pepper sliced
1 potato peeled and cubed
3 tomatoes sliced
3 hard boiled eggs
1/2 head cabbage
2 beef bouillon cubes
salt to taste
oil for frying

Boil the eggs and cut into slices. Fry tortillas until well toasted. Cook ground beef with the potato, bouillon, garlic, onion, salt, and bell pepper. On each totilla place a little of the meat mixture, then cabbage, a slice of egg, and a slice of tomato. Cover with *saksa* abd grated cheese.

Salsa:
2 tomatoes
3 chiles
1 onion
2 cloves garlic
salt
1 bouillon cube
2 tablespoons hot olive oil

(continued)

Enchiladas Catrachas (continued)

Place tomatoes in boiling water for a few minutes, then into cold water to make peeling easy. In blender combine chiles, onion, tomatoes. When blended, add garlic, salt, bouillon cubes and olive oil.

Nicaragua

Tres Leches

1 1/2 cups cake flour
1 teaspoon baking powder
2 cup plus 1 teaspoon sugar
1/2 cup butter softened
5 eggs
1 teaspoon vanilla extract
1 1/3 cups milk
1 cup sweetened condensed milk
1 cup evaporated milk
1 tablespoon light rum
1 cup heavy cream

Preheat oven to 350 degrees. Sift flour and baking powder together. Cream butter and sugar until well blended. Add eggs and 1/2 teaspoon vanilla. Beat until foamy. Gently fold in flour mixture gradually, alternating with 1/3 cup milk.

Pour batter into a lightly greased baking dish, 7 x 11 x 2 inches, and bake for 30 minutes or until a toothpick inserted in the center comes out clean. Cool cake in the pan on wire rack for 20 minutes, then invert onto a serving platter. Pierce the cake with a fork in many places and allow it to cool completely.

Whisk together condensed milk, evaporated milk, 1 cup milk, and rum until well blended. Pour evenly over the cake a little at a time until it is saturated. Refrigerate, covered in plastic wrap for at least 3 hours.

(continued)

Tres Leches (continued)

At serving time whip the heavy cream until it begins to thicken, then add 1 teaspoon sugar and 1/2 teaspoon vanilla and continue whipping until stiff peaks form. Spread cream over the top and sides of the cake with a spatula.

This is outstanding.

Nicaragua

Nacatamales

Masa:
2 cups masa harina
1/2 cup instant mashed potatoes
2 cups milk
1 1/2 teaspoons capers with juice
6 garlic cloves
1 green bell pepper diced
1 onion diced
3/4 pound butter or margarine
1 tablespoon pitted green olives
splash of Tobasco sauce
2 chicken bouillon cubes
1 cup canned tomatoes

Heat milk and dissolve mashed potato in it. Dissolve masa harina in enough water to produce a thick paste and add to milk mixture, then combine other ingredients except butter in a blender. When blended smooth add to thepotato/masa mixture. Melt butter in a large pot and add the dough. Mix and cook until it no longer sticks to the sides of the pot.

Marinate 2 1/2 pounds boneless chicken cut into 20 strips:
    Garlic, cumin, salt, grated onion
    1/4 cup mixed orange and lime juice
Soak in water for 2 hours:
    3/4 pound uncooked rice
    1/2 cup raisins

(continued)

Nacatamales (continued)

Filling:

> 1 pound potatoes peeled and sliced into 20 pieces
> 2 tomatoes sliced into 10 pieces
> 1 onion sliced into 10 pieces
> 1 bell pepper sliced into 10 pieces
> 30 pitted green olives
> 40 capers
> mint

Wrappers:
10 plantain leaves or corn husks, or aluminum foil
twine

Assembly:
Arrange two husks in a T-shape over a one-foot piece of aluminum foil.
Place 1 cup of cooked dough in the center of the wrappers, then the following:

> 3 olives
> 4 capers
> 5 raisins
> 2 strips of chicken
> 1 tablespoon rice
> 2 slices potato
> 1 slice onion
> 1 slice tomato
> small bunch of mint

Close the wrapper carefully over the ingredients. Be sure contents are tightly encased. Tie with twine. Place all ten nacatamales in a large pan or steamer and steam for three hours.

Panamá

Galletas de Frutas

1 cup butter
2 cups sugar
2 eggs
3 cups flour
3 teaspoons baking powder
1/4 teaspoon salt
1/2 teaspoon cloves
2 teaspoons cinnamon
1/2 teaspoon nutmeg
3/4 cup milk
1 cup each pineapple, raisins, candied cherries,
walnuts

Preheat the oven to 350 degrees. Cream the butter and sugar together. Add the eggs one at a time, beating well after each addition. Sift the dry ingredients and add to the mixture alternately with the milk. Add the fruits and distribute them evenly within the dough. Place by tablespoonfuls on a greased cookie sheet, leaving a space of 2 inches between them. Bake 12-15 minutes. Remove from the oven and let cookies rest 10 minutes before removing them from the baking pan.

Panamá

Rice Custard

> 2 cups rice
> 1 can condensed sweetened milk
> 1 can evaporated milk
> 2 cinnamon sticks
> 2 whole cloves
> dash salt
> 2 cups water

Cook the rice in salted water until tender, about 20 minutes. Add remaining ingredients and mix with a fork. Simmer for 15 minutes. Serve warm of cold. For variety, add 1/2 cup pineapple or shredded coconut or raisins.

Mexico

Rosca de Reyes

3 1/2 cups flour
1 package yeast
3/4 cup sugar
7 eggs
1/2 cup butter
1/4 cup lukewarm milk
dash of salt
2 teaspoons cinnamon
1/4 teaspoon anise seed
1 teaspoon vanilla
1/2 cup raisins

Dissolve the yeast in lukewarm milk. Mix yeast, sugar, eggs, melted butter, salt, cinnamon, aniseed, raisins, vanilla, and flour. Knead into a ball. Rub ball with butter, cover and place in a warm spot to rise until it doubles in size—about 2 1/2 hours. Knead on floured board to make dough soft and pliable. Form dough into a *rosca* (ring). Insert a plastic figure somewhere inside the ring of dough to represent the Baby Jesus. Place on a greased baking tray.

Cut into strips:
1/4 cup candied figs
1/4 cup candied orange
1/4 cup candied lemon
1/4 cup candied cherries
1/4 cup candied citron
1 egg beaten
sugar

(continued)

Rosca de Reyes (continued)

Decorate the rosca with candied fruit. Cover and let rise again. Just before baking, brush with beaten egg and sprinkle with sugar. Bake about 40 minutes in a pre-heated oven to 350 degrees.

This is the traditional cake for the Three Kings. Whoever gets the piece with the Baby Jesus is tagged to provide tamales for the next party on February 2.

Mexico

Champurrado

> 6 cups milk
> 1 cup masa harina
> 2 cups water
> 1 cup brown sugar firmly packed
> 3 ounces unsweetened chocolate grated
> 1 cinnamon stick

Heat the milk and chocolate, stirring to dissolve the chocolate. When it is completly dissolved, remove from the heat and set aside to keep warm. Mix the masa harina with the water in another pan, place over low heat, add cinnamon stick, and cook until the mixture has thickened and the masa has become translucent. Add the chocolate milk and sugar. Stir to dissolve the sugar and simmer for a few minutes. Remove the cinnamon stick and serve the champurrado (chocolate atole) hot in mugs.

Chocolate has played a big role in Mexican culture since long before the Spanish got there. Legend says the gods in paradise drank chocolate and the god of the wind brought the seed of the cacao tree as a special blessing to man. It was reported to be the only beverage the Aztec monarch Montezuma would drink.

New Mexico

Most of the foods on Christmas dinner tables in New Mexico are similar—at least in name—to those of the other Spanish-speaking countries. They include *tamales, enchiladas, empanaditas, flan, natillas,* but there is a difference in taste in some items of the same name. It may be the chile, or it may be the piñon nuts, both grown locally. The cuisine is referred to as New Mexican, not Spanish or Mexican. When a diner is asked if he prefers red or green, he knows the question refers to chile, and he sometimes asks for "Christmas," a little of both colors of chile.

Two foods that come from New Mexican kitchens especially at Christmas time are *posole*, a hominy-pork-chile stew, and *biscochitos*, thin, crisp anise-flavored cookies. All the recipes in this section are tried and true—and delicious.

New Mexico

Biscochitos

Dough:
2 cups lard
1 cup sugar
2 eggs
7 level teaspoons anise
6 cups flour
6 level teaspoons baking powder
a little salt

Topping:
1 level tablespoon cinnamon
1 cup sugar

Preheat the oven to 450 degrees. Place lard in mixing bowl; add sugar and eggs. Mix well for about two minutes with an electric beater. Mix flour, baking powder, and salt, then add to lard mixture. Mix well. Knead the dough until it forms the shape of a ball. Roll it out on a lightly floured board to about 1/8 inch thickness. Cut the cookies with a cookie cutter. Spread cinnamon and sugar topping evenly on the cookies. Bake 10 to 12 minutes. Let cool thoroughly.

The texture and taste of the cookies will be affected if you use a shortening other than lard. It is the lard that gives them their melt-in-your-mouth "shortness."

In 1989 the New Mexico Legislature declared the biscochito the official state cookie.

New Mexico

Abad's Posole

1 pound dry posole (try posole with white, blue, and yellow corn=colorful and tasty)
1 1/2 – 2 pounds pork stew meat cut into 1-inch cubes and browned in 1 – 2 tablepoons lard or hot oil
1 large white onion chopped
12 cloves garlic chopped
16 ounce can of diced tomatos
1/2 tablespoon dried oregano
32 ounces chicken broth
3 quarts water
1/2 – 3/4 tablespoon brown sugar
2 – 4 tablespoons red chile powder or 6 – 10 pods dry red chile
salt to taste

Combine chicken broth, water, pork stew meat, and dry posole and bring to a boil. After ingredients begin to boil, cover and reduce to medium heat. Add chopped garlic, canned tomatoes, dried oregano, and chile powder, and simmer for about 2 1/2 hours. Add onion, brown sugar, and salt, and cook for another 1 – 1 1/2 hours, depending on the consistency you like. (Abad: I like mine a little on the crunchy side,) Adjust the seasonings. Top with grated Cheddar cheese. Serve with flour tortillas.

New Mexico

Natillas

> 4 eggs separated
> 1/4 cup flour
> 4 cups milk
> 3/4 cup sugar
> 1/4 teaspoon salt
> nutmeg
> cinnamon

Place egg yolks, flour, and 1 cup of milk in small bowl. Stir to make a smooth paste. Set aside. Place the remaining milk, sugar, and salt in a pan and scald at medium heat. Add the egg mixture to the scalded milk and continue to cook at medium heat until a soft custard consistency is reached. Remove from heat and allow to cool to room temperature. Beat the egg whites until they are stiff but not dry. Fold egg whites into the custard. Chill and sprinkle with nutmeg and cinnamon.

New Mexico

Sopa

1 cup sugar
1/2 teaspoon vanilla
1/2 teaspoon cinnamon
6 to 8 slices homemade white bread toasted
3 tablespooons butter
1 cup raisins
1 cup chopped apple
1/2 pound longhorn cheese grated
1/2 cup piñon nuts

Melt sugar over high heat, stirring for about 4 minutes or until it is a deep caramel color. Remove from heat and add 1 cup of water carefully in a slow stream. Return to heat and stir until sugar is dissolved, then add vanilla and cinnamon. Simmer 1 minute. Spread bread slices with butter and arrange in layers in a buttered square 8-inch baking pan. Sprinkle bread with raisins, nuts, and apple, then with cheese. Pour syrup over all and bake in preheated 350 degree oven for 30 minutes. Serve warm.

New Mexico

Empanadas

Filling:
1 1/2 pound boiling meat: beef, pork, or tongue (tongue is
traditional)
1 cup raisins or currants
1 cup sugar
1/4 cup dark corn syrup or molasses
4 teaspoons ground cinnamon
1 teaspoon salt
4 cups piñon nuts or walnuts
1 cup sherry or other wine, bourbon, or brandy

Simmer meat until tender, then grind or chop finely and combine
with other ingredients. Filling should be thick and moist, not dry. If dry,
moisten with more wine.

Dough:
2 tablespoons lard
4 cups flour
1 teaspoon salt
1 teaspoon baking powder
about 1 1/2 cups water

Mix flour and lard together until consistency of corn meal. Add
other dry ingredients, mixing well. Add water slowly, mixing until dough
is about the consistency of pie crust dough. Roll out into rounds about 4
inches in diameter and 1/8-inch thick. Place 1 to 3 tablespoons filling in
the middle of the found, leaving edges clean for sealing. Fold in half and

(continued)

Empanadas (continued)

seal by wetting the inside edges with a very small amount of milk or egg
white and pressing edges gently with a fork. Deep fry until golden brown.
Drain on paper towels. If you resist fried foods, try baking them at 350
degrees. Let cool. Serve at room temperature.

New Mexico

Tamales

2 pounds dried corn husks for wrapping tamales. Cover with hot water and soak for 2 hours or until tender.

Meat filling (chile con carne)
2 pounds lean pork
2 pounds lean beef
2 tablespoons fat, lard, or salad oil
2 tablespoons flour
1 tablespoons salt
2 cloves garlic
2 cups prepared red chile sauce
4 cups cold water
pinch of oregano
pinch of cumin

Cut meat into inch-size pieces. Braise in the fat or oil; add garlic, flour, and salt. Stir well. When the meat is braised, add the chile sauce diluted with water, cumin, and oregano. Simmer until tender, an hour or more. Remove garlic when the meat is done. Cool thoroughly.

Dough (Masa):
1 1/2 cups lard
6 pounds masa harina
1 tablespoon salt
1 cup water
2 tablespoons baking powder

(continued)

Tamales (continued)

Whip the lard to the consistency of whipped cream. Mix in the masa. Add salt and baking powder and beat until fluffy so that a little dropped into water will float to the top. If the masa is too dry to spread easily on the corn husks, add a little more water and beat again.

To roll the tamales, spread a corn husk flat. Place 1 rounded tablespoon of masa (about the size of a large egg) in the center of the corn husk and mold into a rectangular shape about 3
inches by 1 inch. Place 1 tablespoon chile mixture in the center. Bring corn husk sides together, covering masa well. Tie ends with corn husk strips. Place tamales in a steamer and cover with a tight lid. Steam for 45 minutes. Remove husks before eating. Serve with red or green chile.

New Mexico

Abad's Green Chile Stew

1 1/2 pounds pork stew meat
32 ounces chicken broth
4 – 5 medium potatoes pre-baked to a medium
consistency
1 large white onion chopped
10 cloves garlic chopped
16-ounce can diced tomatoes
16 ounces precooked pinto beans
12 medium hot, roasted, peeled, chopped green chiles
(more if desired)
Salt to taste

Cut pork stew meat into 1/2-inch squares and brown in 1 tablespoon oil. Combine chicken broth and two quarts of water. Add pork, cover, and cook on medium heat for 30 minutes. Cut potatoes into 1/2-inch cubes. Add onion, garlic, potatoes, beans, and green chiles. Add salt to taste and cook on medium heat for about 1 hour. Serve with flour tortillas or sopaipillas.

New Mexico

Chile Caribe

1 medium round steak cut into small cubes
2 dozen red chile pods, stems and most seeds removed
2 cloves garlic or more to taste
pinch of oregano
salt to taste
1/4 cup catsup

Brown meat in a little oil in a heavy skillet. Cover and let it tenderize, adding small amounts of water if necessary. Preheat oven to 325 degrees, then place chile pods on cookie sheet. Roast carefully for 3 or 4 minutes until they smell roasted but not burned. Rinse chiles, place in large pan, and cover with water. Cook 5 minutes until tender. Place 6-8 pods at a time, garlic, and a little water in blender. Blend until very smooth, adding more liquid if necessary. Pour blended chile into pan with meat. Add salt, catsup, oregano, and cook on low heat, uncovered for 1 to 2 hours. Use this for enchiladas, burritos, chile, or other favorite New Mexican dishes.

New Mexico

Chile Colorado

> 2 tablespoons shortening
> 4 tablespoons flour
> 1/2 to 1 cup red chile powder (to taste)
> 4 cups cold water
> 1 teaspoon garlic salt
> 1/2 teaspoon salt
> 1/2 teaspoon oregano
> 1/4 teaspoon cumin

Heat shortening, add flour, and cook for 1 minute. Add chile powder and cook an additional minute. Gradually add the water and stir, making sure no lumps form. Add all remaining ingredients and simmer for 15 to 20 minutes.

This can be stored in the refrigerator or frozen. With the addition of a pound or two of cooked beef or pork, it become *chile con carne*.

New Mexico

Chile Verde

       2 tablespoons shortening
       1 cup chopped onion
       4 tablespoons flour

       2 cups chopped green chile
       2 cups chicken broth
       1/2 teaspoon garlic powder
       1/2 teaspoon salt

Heat shortening and sauté chopped onion. Add flour and cook for one minute. Add all other ingredients and simmer 20 minutes. Cooked beef or pork may be added.

Glossary

Abrazo	embrace.
Abuelo/a	grandfather, grandmother; plays role of bogeyman in *Oremos, Los Matachines* in New Mexico.
Aguinaldo	Christmas song; Christmas gift; small bags or baskets of candy, nuts, other sweets; small gift usually of cash to employees; in *Oremos* children going door to door asking for treats.
Aire libre	open air; outside.
Alumbrado	lighted, illuminated; used in reference to *el día de las velitas,* the festival of lights, in Colombia on December 7.
Angelito	little angel.
Árbol de Navidad	Christmas tree.
Árbol de pascuas	Christmas tree.
Arroz con dulce	sweet rice dish.
Asalto	literally assault; pre-planned "assault" on the host of a Christmas party at the end of a *parranda.*
Autos sacramentales	acts of faith; sacred ordinances; liturgical religious plays from medieval Spain, still observed in New Mexico.
Baile	dance.
Bebido	drink.
Belén	Bethlehem.
El Belén	*nacimiento, portal;* Christmas nativity scene.

Biscochitos	crisp, anise-flavored Christmas cookies of New Mexico.
Bonos Navideños	bonuses of one month's salary, Costa Rica.
Brindis	toasts.
Los bundes	dance, traditional post-Christmas festivities in Panamá.
Buñuelos	pastry made of flour, eggs, butter, and milk; rolled out like tortilla, fried and sprinkled with cinnamon and sugar.
La cabañuela	folk method used to predict weather of the new year.
Cabo a rabo	head to toe; start to finish; in Costa Rica term used to describe house cleaning for the new year.
Caja china	literally China box; barbecue pit for *el lechón asado*.
Calenda	procession.
Campesinos	countrymen, peasants.
Canastas navideñas	Christmas baskets, gifts given to employees, service people.
Cancha	field; track; open air market at *feria navideña* in Argentina.
Candelero	candlestick, oil lamp; used in Feast of Candelaria forty days after Christmas, February 2.
La caridad	charity, gifts for the needy.
La carne frita	fried meat.
Cena	supper, evening meal.
Cerveza	beer.
Charango	5-string Andean guitar.
Chicharrones	crisp, fried pork rind.

Chichi	corn whiskey.
Chiribiscos	dry sticks of wood collected by children in Guatemala for la *quema del Diablo*. Guatemala.
Chicote	whip carried by *abuelos* in New Mexico.
Chocolo	corncob.
Chocolatadas	Christmas events in Peru where hot chocolate and panettone are served.
Clerico	chilled Christmas punch.
Cochinitos de aguinaldo	plastic pigs placed in prominent places to receive *aguinaldos*, gifts of money, for the needy.
Cocotero	coconut palm.
Los Comanchitos	Christmas play in New Mexico in which "Comanches" steal a child; villagers pursue and rescue the child for a ransom.
Coquito	coconut pudding.
El corazón limpio	clean heart; in Panamá after *el espiritu de la Navidad*, a time to pray for all things hoped for.
Corridas de toro	Costa Rican nod to Spanish bull fights; bull is never injured; activity to get rid of old year's frustrations.
Criollos	Creoles; persons of European descent born in the Americas.
Cupil	headdress worn in *Los Matachines*.
Dando los días	literally giving the days; honoring all those named Manuel or Manuela in New Mexico on January 1,

Danza de los cintos	dance of the ribbons.
Dar las pascuas	to wish happy holiday, merry Christmas.
Dar y no recibir	to give and not to receive; a *juego de aguinaldo*.
La Desaparición del Niño Jesús	disappearance of the Baby Jesus; image of the Baby is hidden, and villagers search for it; event between December 26 and December 30; Honduras.
Despedida del año	farewell to the old year.
Día de las madres	mothers day, celebrated on December 8, in honor of the Immaculate Virgin.
Día de la Virgen Immaculada	feast day of the Immaculate Virgin.
Día de locos y locainos	Day of the "crazies" December 28, when tricks are played on friends, roles are reversed; Venezuela.
Día de los inocentes	Day of the Innocents December 28, time for tricks and jokes.
Día de los niños	Day of the children, Three Kings Day January 6.
Día de los velitas	December 7 in Colombia, eve of *la Virgen Immaculada*, also *el alumbrado*.
Día de Reyes	also *día de los Reyes*; Three Kings Day.
Doble sueldo	an extra month's salary.
Dulce desayuno	breakfast of sweets.
Empanada	pastry filled with meat or fruit.
Enano	dwarf; dancing partner of *la gigantona* in Nicaragua.
Encomendero	Spanish colonist in charge of *encomiendas*.

Encomienda	system practiced in Spanish colonial times in which an *encomendero* was responsible for the protection and welfare of a group of Indians who, in turn, worked for him.
Entrega de varas	entrance of the officials, Perú, January 1, a time to pass the wooden scepter of authority from the old leader to the new.
Espíritu de la Navidad	spirit of Christmas, in Panamá a time for reflection and repentance before observing *el corazón limpio*.
Estancia	ranch.
Estrella de Navidad	Christmas star.
Estrellita	fireworks; also *silbador, mortero*.
Farolitos	small lanterns; in New Mexico paper sacks with candles.
Felicidades	good wishes, congratulations.
Feliz Navidad	Merry Christmas.
Feria navideña	Christmas fair in Bolivia.
Feria santurantikuy	market in Perú for selling Christmas saints.
Fiesta de mono	fiesta in which a monkey is the chief character.
Fiesta del año viejo	fiesta of the old year.
Finca	farm, property.
Fin de año	end of the year.
Flor de pascua	holiday flower; poinsettia.
Flor de pastor	*flor de pascua*; poinsettia.

Fogón	hearth.
Gaita	Venezuelan song, originally a song of protest, now using more themes.
Gaita zuliana	*gaita* from the state of Zulia in Venezuela; uses Christmas themes.
Gaitero	leader of a *gaita* group.
Galletas	cookies.
Garifuna	black Carib of northern Honduras.
Gaucho	cowboy in South America.
Gauchupines	disrespectful term for *peninsulares*, persons born in Europe.
La gigantona	giant puppet on stilts, 12 feet high, representing queen, symbol of *la Virgen María*, dances with *enano* in Nicaragua.
Los globos elevar	to make the balloons ascend.
La gritería	the calling; in Nicaragua on December 7, beginning of Christmas celebration; at first a shout, then general uproar, finally loud singing.
Habichuelas	pinto beans in Puerto Rico.
Hallaca	traditional Venezuelan tamales.
Hojuelas	Colombian pastry; see buñuelos.
Hosteleros	innkeepers.
El indio bárbaro	the bearded Indian; in Honduras the bringer of gifts on Christmas Day among the Garifuna.

Inkarri	one of the Three Kings, otherwise known as Melchior; the Inca king; arriving in Perú in horse-drawn cart.
Jefe de los locos	chief of the "crazies"; Venezuela.
Jíbaro	mountain-dwelling people in Puerto Rico.
Joncanu	also John Canoe; Wanaragua , dance of the warriors, in Honduras and other parts of Central America.
Juegos	games.
Lechón	suckling pig.
Lechón asado	roasted lechón.
Llonque	sugarcane ale.
Luminarias	bonfires to light the way to Bethlehem. Sometimes there are three to signify the Holy Family or twelve for the apostles; probably of pagan origin to celebrate rituals of the gods; also used by shepherds to keep warm and to frighten away wild animals; used especially in New Mexico Christmas celebrations.
Manjar blanco	Colombian pudding.
La marranada	New Year's tradition in Colombia of group roasting and eating of a pig.
Máscaro	masked.
Los Matachines	dance drama in New Mexico.
Merengue	popular Caribbean dance.
Misa de gallo	also *misa del gallo*; mass of the rooster; midnight mass on Christmas Eve; so named because legend says the rooster was the first to announce the birth of Christ.

Mis crismas	my Christmas treats; common in New Mexico.
Los misterios	the Holy Family as seen in *nacimientos*.
Mistirri	one of the Three Kings, Gaspar, king of the mestizos; these kings arrive in a horse-drawn cart; Peru.
Montería	leftovers from *la cena de Nochebuena*.
Moros y cristianos	Moors and Christians literally; a signature dish of beans and rice in Cuba.
Morteros	fireworks.
Muñecos	dolls, puppets.
Nacimiento	scene depicting the birth of Christ; also *portal, Belén pasito*, creche; usually displayed from December 16 until January 6.
Natilla, Natillas	pudding.
La Navidad	gift of money from Ecuadorian employers to their employees.
La Navidad de los pobres	Christmas of the poor; in Ecuador when rural workers bring gifts to their patrones and ask for la Navidad.
Navidades	things relating to Christmas.
Negrorri	one of the Three Kings, Balthasar, the black king, arriving in horse-drawn cart.; Peru.
Niño Dios	Baby Jesus. Child of God.
Niño Manuelito	Baby Jesus, Emmanuel.
Niños envueltos	literally wrapped up children; a type of stuffed cabbage.
Nochebuena	Christmas Eve.

Novena	nine days of prayer for a particular subject; *novena del Niño, novena de aguinaldos.*
Octavitas	eight days following Three Kings Day, featuring *parrandas* and general festivity.
Olla	literally pot.
Oremos	Christmas activity in New Mexico.
Padrinazgo	godparent sponsorship.
La palma	scepter carried by *matacin* dancers in New Mexico.
Palo volador	pole flyer, Honduras; person climbs 40 foot pole, ties rope around his body, then descends as the rope unwinds.
La palomita	old Spanish dance.
Pan de jamón	ham-stuffed pastry.
Pan dulce	sweet bread.
Papá Noel, Papá Noë	Father Christmas.
Parranda	party, with lots of drinking, eating, singing, dancing.
Parrandero	participant in the *parranda*, "party aimal."
Pasada	shelter; resting place.
Pascua	term used for holidays, especially Easter and Christmas.
Pascua de los Negros	Christmas of the Blacks.
Pase del Niño Viajero	passing (parade) of the wandering Child, a special image in Ecuador.
Paseo de olla	procession of the pot; Colombian tradition of viewing muñecos and taking along a large olla of *sancocho* for an extended family outdoor feast.

Pasito	*nacimiento.*
Pasteles	pies.
Pastelito	little pie.
Pastorcitos	little shepherds.
Pastorela	shepherds play.
Los Pastores	*auto sacramentale* performed in New Mexico.
Patinadores	roller skaters.
Peninsulares	persons born in Europe, living in the Americas.
Los peregrinos	pilgrims.
El pesebre	*nacimiento.*
El pesebre viviente	living *nacimiento.*
Picadita	cold cuts, cheeses, etc. to serve as starters, appetizers, Uruguay.
La piñata	hollow pot or ball filled with candies, to be broken with a stick by blindfolded children.
Pino de Navidad	Christmas tree.
Pisco	Peruvian brandy.
Pitos	small whistles, flutes.
Plato navideño	Christmas menu.
Pobres	the poor.
Portal	*nacimiento.*

Posole	a soup made of hominy and pork, popular at Christmas time in Mexico and New Mexico.
Procesión del Niño	parade, procession honoring the Baby Jesus.
Pupusas	stuffed, grilled tortillas, common in Central America.
La Purísima	feast of the Immaculate Conception.
La quema del Diablo	burning of the devil in Guatemala at 6 p.m. on December 7, symbolizing repentance and purification.
Quena	notched, open-ended flute.
Rábanos	radishes; over-sized radishes carved into exotic shapes, Oaxaca, Mexico.
Repartimiento	a system of labor forced on the natives by the Spanish, similar to *encomiendo*.
Robo y búsqueda	stealing and searching for the Baby Jesus in the days following Christmas—always ending in a party when the search is successful.
Ron	rum.
Ropatón	eggnog-like punch.
Rosca de Reyes	ring of the kings; special cake made for Three Kings Day in the shape of a ring; plastic figure of Baby Jesus hidden inside; finder to host a party on Candlemas, February 2, celebrating presentation of Jesus in the temple.
San José	St. Joseph.
San Juan de los caballeros	name given by Oñate to his first settlement in New Mexico, near today's Oke Owinge pueblo.
Sancocho	a vegetable soup especially traditional in Colombia.

Santo Niño	Holy Child.
Sidra	cider.
Silbadores	fireworks; see *estrellita, montero*.
Sopa paraguaysa	spoon bread from Paraguay.
Tamales	universal favorite; various stuffings enclosed in masa and wrapped in cornhusks or banana leaves.
Tambleque	drink based on coconut milk.
Tepeyec	hill in Mexico where *la Virgen María* appeared to Juan Diego.
Tica Linda	queen of *el tope* parade in Costa Rica.
Tilma	cape of *la Virgen de Guadalupe* that she gave Juan Diego to show as a sign to the bishop; when opened, fresh roses fell from it.
Tonada	song.
El tope	fiestas, grand horse show and parade in Costa Rica.
Los Tres Magos, Tres Reyes	January 6, the Day of the Epiphany, Three Kings Day, Three Wise Men.
Los tripas morcillas	blood pudding.
Trulla	a growing crowd of revelers and musicians who parade In the streets, ending in an *asalto* on a pre-planned host.
Turrones	nougat-like candy.
Vieja Belén	old lady of Bethlehem who visits poor children after Christmas.

Viejo pascuero	the old man who brings Christmas gifts, Santa Claus; Chile; even without snow he arrives with his team of reindeer.
Villancico	Christmas song, from medieval Europe; usually has serious, religious theme.
Virgen María	the Virgin Mary.
Víspera	vespers, day before religious event.
Wanaragua	dance of the warriors, Honduras; *joncanu*; John Canoe.
Yuca frita	fried cassava.
Zampoña	Andean flute.

Bibliography

Books

Allende, Heraclito Vivance, *Album 17, Villancicos Quechuas del Folklore Peruano*. Lima: Libreria, Imporador, 1977.

Alvarez, Julia, *The Secret Footprints*. New York: Knopf, 2000.

Arbeau, Thoinot, *Orchesography*. C. W. Beaumont, 1925.

Bannon, John F., ed., *Bolton and the Spanish Borderlands*. Norman, OK: University of Oklahoma Press, 1964.

Beck, Peggy V., *Oremos, Oremos: New Mexican Midwinter Masquerade*. Taos: Millicent Rogers Museum, 1987.

Bolton, Herbert Eugene, *Coronado Knight of Pueblos and Plains*. Albuquerque: UNM Press, 1949.

Castro, Rafaela G., *Chicano Folklore, a Guide to the Folktales, Traditions, Rituals and Religious Practices of Mexican Americans*. New York: Oxford University Press, 2001.

Catena, Osvaldo, *Villancicos tradicionales argentinos*. Buenos Aires: Editorial Bonum, 1975.

Challis, Evelyn, ed., *Songs for a New Generation, Jumping, Laughing and Resting*. New York: Oak Publications, 1974.

Champe, Flavia Waters, *The Matachines Dance of the Upper Rio Grande*. Lincoln: University of NE, 1983.

Chase, Gilbert, *The Music of Spain*. New York: Dover Publications, 1959.

Chavez, Thomas, *New Mexico Past and Future*. Albuquerque: UNM Press, 2006.

Claro, Samuel, *Antología de la música colonial en América del Sur*. Santiago: Ediciones de la Universidad de Chile, n.d.

De Gainza, Violeta H. and Guillermo Graetzer, *Canten señores cantores: 150 melodias del cancionero tradicional*. Buenos Aires: Ricordi Americana S.A.E.C., 1963.

De Saettone, Mary Rose, ed. *Nochebuena y Navidad: Eleven Carols from Latin America*. Delaware, OH: Cooperative Recreation Service, 1961.

Delacre, Lulu, Las Navidades: *Popular Christmas Songs from Latin America*. New York: Scholastic Press, 1990.

D'León, Prof. David, *La educacion musical en la expresion artística*. Mexico City, 1997.

Espinosa, Aurelio M., *The Folklore of Spain in the American Southwest: Traditional Spanish Folk Literature in Northern New Mexico and Southern* Colorado. Norman, OK: University of OK, 1990.

Floriano, Antonio C., *El Monasterio de Santa María de Guadalupe*. Coruña-León: Editorial Everest—Carraterro León, n.d.

Fuson, Robert J., tr., *The Log of Christopher Columbus*. Camden, ME: International Marine Publications, 1987.

Hernández, Luis Alberto de León, *Organización de agrupaciones corales*. Puerto Rico: Departamento de Instrucción Pública, 1981.

Jaramillo, Cleofas M., *Shadows of the Past*. Santa Fe: Ancient City Press, n.d.

Kanellos, Nicolás, ed., *Noche Buena: Hispanic American Christmas Stories*. Oxford University Press, 2000.

Lamadrid, Enrique R., *Tesoros del Espíritu: A Portrait in Sound of Hispanic New Mexico*. Embudo, NM: El Norte Academia Publications, 1994.

_____ , *Hermanitos Comanchitos*. Albuquerque: UNM Press, 2003.

Lloyd, A. L. and Isabel Aretz de Ramón y Rivera, *Folk Songs of the Americas.* New York: International Folk Music Council, n.d.

Loeffler, Jack, *Hispano Folk Music of the Rio Grande del Norte.* Albuquerque: UNM Press, 1999.

Luce, Allena, ed., *Songs of Spain and of the Americas.* Boston: D. C. Heath, 1946.

Miller, Carl S., ed., *Rockabye Baby: Lullabies of Many Lands and Peoples.* New York: Chappel Music Co., 1975.

Montaño, Mary, *Tradiciones Nuevomejicanas: Hispano Arts and Culture of New Mexico.* Albuquerque: UNM Press, 2001.

Nusom, Lynn, *Christmas in New Mexico: Recipes, Traditions and Folklore for the Holiday Season.* Phoenix: Golden West Publishing Co., 1991.

Orsi, Luis Salazar, *100 rondas infantiles.* Lima: Tarea de Publicaciones Educativas, 1993.

Ortega, Pedro Ribera, *Christmas in Old Santa Fe.* Santa Fe: Sunstone Press, 1973.

Palarea, Alvaro Fernaud, ed., *Cuadernos de cultura popular: melodias tradicionales para uso escolar.* Caracas: Consejo Nacional de la Cultura CONAC, 1988.

Pillsbury, Dorothy L. *Star Over Adobe.* Albuquerque: UNM Press, 1986.

Posada-Charrúa, José and Hiltraud Reckmann, *Navidad: Sudamerikanische Weinachtslieder.* Spabrüken: Soon Edition Marita Kubitzki, n.d.

Presilla, Marciel E., *Feliz Nochebuena, Feliz Navidad: Christmas Feasts of the Hispanic Caribbean.* New York: Henry Holt, n.d.

Reeve, Frank and Alice Ann Cleaveland, *New Mexico Land of Many Cultures.* Boulder: Parrott Publishing Co., 1969.

Rios, María Alvarez and María Antonieta, *Cantos infantiles cubanos.* Havana: Instituto Cubano del Libro, 2000.

Roberts, Susan A. and Calvin A. Roberts, *A History of New Mexico*. Albuquerque: UNM Press, 1986.

Rodriguez, Sylvia, *The Matachines Dance: Ritual Symbolism and Interethnic Relations in the Upper Rio Grande Valley*. Albuquerque: UNM Press, 1996.

Stark, Richard M., *Music of the Spanish Folk Plays in New Mexico*. Santa Fe: Museum of New Mexico Press, 1969.

Torres, Larry, *Six Nuevomexicano Folk Dramas for Advent Season*. Albuquerque: UNM Press, 1999.

_____, *Yo Seigo de Taosi: Ensayos Culturales Nuevo Mexicanos*. Taos: El Crepúsculo, 1992.

Villagra, Gaspar Perez de, tr. by Gilberto Espinosa, *A History of New Mexico*. Albuquerque: Rio Grande Press, 1933.

Wakefield, Charito Calvachi, *Navidad Latinoamericana*. Elizabethtown, PA: Latin American Creations, 2001.

Weigle, Marta and Peter White, *The Lore of New Mexico*. Albuquerque: UNM Press, 1988.

Wernecke, Herbert, *Celebrating Christmas Around the World*. Philadelphia: Westminster Press, 1962.

White-Lea, Aurora Lucero, *Literary Folklore of the Hispanic Southwest*. San Antonio: The Naylor Co., 1957.

Reference Books

De Gámea, Tana, editor in chief, *Simon and Schuster's International Dictionary, English/Spanish*. New York: Simon and Schuster, n.d.

Dubois-Charlier, Françoise, project editor. *The American Heritage Spanish Dictionary*. Boston: Houghton Mifflin, 1986.

Gradante, William, "Aguinaldos," *The New Grove Dictionary of Music and Musicians*, Stanley Sadie, ed. London: MacMillan, 1991.

Pope, Isabel and Thomas Stanford, "Villancicos." *The New Grove Dictionary of Music and Musicians*, Stanley Sadie, ed. London: MacMillan, 1991.

Internet

Bermúdez, Egberto, "El Villancico de Navidad, Variantes Coloniales de una Tradición profana y religiosa Española." Internet: http://www/banrep.Gov.co/blaavirtual/credencial/hvillan.htm.

Cohen, Jonathan, "The Naming of America: Fragments We've Shored Against Ourselves." Internet: http://www.uhmc.sunysb.edu/surgery/america.html.

Devlin, Wendy, "History of the Piñata," Mexico Connect, Internet: http://www.mexconnect.com/mex_/travel/wdevlin/wdpinatahistory.html.

El tesoro de la lengua castellana o español, Internet: Wikipedia.

King, Judy, "Christmas Holidays in Mexico: Festivals and Light, Love, and Peace," Internet: King, Judy.

"Los Aguinaldos, deliciosas sorpresas de Navidad." Internet: http://www.elcolombiano.com.co/proyectos/navidad2001/navidenas/losaguinaldos.htm.

Oetgen, Susan K., "A Short History of the Colonial Villancicos of New Spain," Latin American Folk Institute. Internet: http://www.lafi.org/Magazine/articles/villancico.html.

"Sebastian de Covarrubias," Internet: Wikipedia.

Valdivielso Arce, Jaime, "La Postulación de los Aguinaldos una Costumbre Popular," Revista de Folklore, numero 158. Internet

Articles

Lujan, Alfredo Celedon, "Mis Crismas." Santa Fe *New Mexican*, 12/22/02.

"The Días." Taos: Millicent Rogers Museum, n.d.

Correspondence/Interviews

Abril, Carlos (Cuba) Northwestern University.

Arana, Patricia, Uruguay.

Elduayen David, (Ecuador, Venezuela) Alexandria, VA.

Gonzales, Juan de Dios (Bolivia) Glendale, CA.

Graetzer, Dina, Buenos Aires, Argentina.

Gutierrez, Digna (Nicaragua) Albuquerque.

Humphrey, Carolina, Dominican Republic.

Lopez-Ibor, Sofía (Spain) San Francisco

Martinez, Cecilia, Oaxaca, Mexico.

Park, Susan, Perú.

Posada, Pilar, Medellin, Colombia.

Index

LaVergne, TN USA
13 December 2009
166863LV00002B/10/P